SEVEN PORTALS TO YOUR SOUL

An Accessible Guide for Mending Your Life

Marcia A. Phillips

Bridges of Unity  Loves Park, Illinois

Seven Portals To Your Soul
An Accessible Guide for Mending Your Life
by Marcia A. Phillips

Published by:
Bridges of Unity
Post Office Box 15727
Loves Park, IL 61132 U.S.A.

Phone / Fax 1-815-636-2867
orders@bridgesofunity.com
www.bridgesofunity.com

Cover Design: Peter Massari
Interior Art: Brett Phillips

ISBN 0-9759030-0-4

Library of Congress Control Number: 2004094744

Manufactured in the United States of America

Dedication

In Appreciation

For your courage to live a physical life
For the lessons you have given and received
For the healing contributions you have made
And for the unique spark of your souls…

This book is dedicated to all who have called our beloved Earth their home.

About the Author

Marcia A. Phillips is a visionary, intuitive healer, bodyworker, teacher, and author. She holds an unwavering vision of a world that works together as One, collaborating for the best and highest good of all.

Marcia left corporate America in 1997, after a year of being prompted by her Higher Self to work with others in the healing realm. She received a strong vision to become an author of spiritual self-help books, as well as a healer, speaker, and teacher in that area.

Marcia's abilitiy to explain difficult concepts in everyday language stems from her many years of teaching adults and high school students. As technical training manager and materials engineer for a Fortune 500 company, she initiated new training techniques that helped the technical and non-technical sales force to more easily understand and sell the latest technical equipment and processes.

Marcia has degrees from the University of Wisconsin (Home Economics Education), and Rutgers, the State University of New Jersey (Ceramic Engineering). She is a registered and nationally certified massage therapist, and a continuous student of life's everyday experiences.

In this book, Marcia offers the reader the step-by-step process that she has discovered and employed to mend her life. These are the same techniques she uses with her clients to bring more joy, healing, and peace to their lives. The mother of two grown children, Marcia is living the life of her dreams with her beloved partner Ron, in Northern Illinois.

Contents

Exercises

Acknowledgments

My love and gratitude go out to the hundreds of people who have assisted me in learning my life lessons. They are foundational to the writing of this book. A special thanks goes to my parents, children, partner, ex-husband, siblings, friends, and clients. Most of the stories in this book are true. The names of the individuals involved have been changed to protect their privacy.

Becoming a published author has been my dream for many years. There are certain people who help us hold our dreams. They have the ability to compassionately allow us to be as we are while encouraging us to be all we are meant to be. Their unconditional love helps us to flourish. My partner Ron, my son Brett, and my daughter Jen are three such people in my life. Your courage to live your truth is an inspiration. For your presence, your constancy, your support, and your love, I am forever grateful. You add incredible joy and depth to my life.

Several people stepped up to the plate and offered their gifts to help bring this book into publication. They are listed below. There is one person in particular who gave me his support and editorial assistance from beginning to end. A University of Wisconsin Professor Emeritus, he authored numerous professional books and articles, and was the editor of two prestigious educational journals. His love, encouragement, wisdom, and attention to detail are deeply appreciated. Thank you, Dad.

L. Joseph Lins, Ph.D. – Editorial Assistance
Robert J. Lins, M.D. – Meditations
Peter Massari – Cover Design
Brett Phillips – Interior Art
Portrait by Ron

You Are In Charge

No one else can mend our lives for us. If life isn't working, it is up to us to do something about it. We are each ultimately in charge of our own lives.

There are many ways of mending one's life. It is important to follow one's inner counsel regarding what works. It may be a combination of things such as alternative and complementary therapies, western medicine, diet, exercise, psychotherapy, and spiritual pursuits. This book is not meant to give you the only way to mend your life. I hope it assists you on your journey.

Although I tend to approach my physical problems from a spiritual point of view, I am not recommending that you avoid medical treatment or stop the treatments you are currently using for any mental, emotional, or physical problems you may have. Each of us must decide for ourselves the best methods to use for our spiritual and physical healing. It is my hope that the exercises in this book will complement and enhance the other healing modalities that work for you.

Each of us has a unique perspective on life. This book represents mine at the present time. Pure truth is quite rare in this world. Most of what we think is true is veiled in illusion. It is not important to have a firm grasp on "absolute truth". That is not the purpose of this existence. Of greater import is to share our perceptions and discover a greater awareness together. What I have written contains perceptions, images, and exercises that have been helpful to me in understanding and healing my chakras and mending my life.

Therefore, rather than holding onto the concepts or words in this book (or any teaching) as "absolute truth", or rather than rejecting them altogether because they do not quite fit, I encourage you to use them as a catalyst to find your own truth in the moment. Then allow that truth to evolve, as it will. You are in charge.

—Marcia A. Phillips

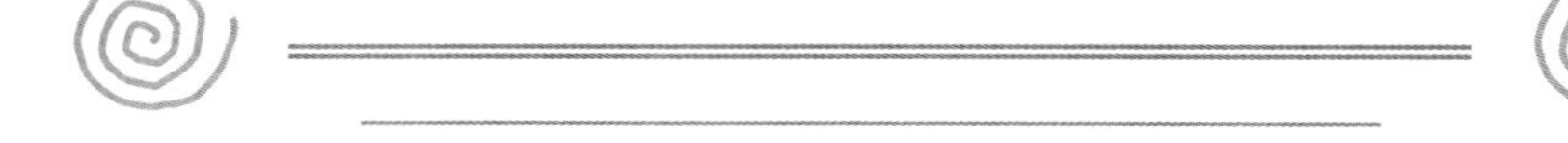

Are You Soaring With Your Soul...

We are in the shadow of something grand.

To see it takes a shift in perspective.

This book will help you to make that shift.

ARE YOU SOARING WITH YOUR SOUL...

Or Is Your Life Less Than Wonderful?

Do you love your life? Do you greet each morning with enthusiasm? Are you passionate about what you do? Are you surrounded by loving and supportive people? Do you have what you need to live comfortably? Do you feel really good about yourself, inside and out? Is your life the life of your dreams? If you can answer *yes* to all of these questions, then you may already be soaring with your soul. You will find this book to be an inspiring and helpful enhancement to your already wonderful life.

If, however, your answer to any of the above questions was *no*, what seems to be the problem? Are you having a hard time keeping up with the frantic pace, and feeling worn out? Are you worried about your ability to support yourself and your family? Are you frustrated because the same painful situations or relationships keep happening to you again and again? Are you feeling confused and anxious about the future? Do you feel badly about yourself or your choices in life? Is there something about your life that you wish you could change? If your answer to any of these questions is *yes*, then this book is definitely for you! The information and exercises in it are designed to help you:

- **Reduce your stress and find peace**
- **Resolve your internal struggles**
- **Find healing and wisdom through your negative encounters and relationships**
- **Make choices that support you**
- **End destructive patterns**
- **Live with greater ease and awareness**
- **Take back your power**
- **Love your life and yourself more**

Thousands feel as if their lives have been turned upside down. They've lost their jobs, homes, life savings, or close loved ones. Fear, uncertainty, and feelings of loneliness and isolation abound. People around the world are steeped in suffering. Many are wondering where all this will end. Some are on the verge of throwing in the towel.

For many people, it feels like the world is going faster, but their lives are going nowhere. They go through the motions each day, falling into bed at night exhausted. They wake up tired the next morning, wishing they could somehow stop the endless gerbil wheel they call life. They wonder, "What's the point; why am I here; and is there anything I can do to change this?"

That's where I was seven years ago. I woke up one morning realizing I either had to take back my life, or it would take me. The life force was being siphoned right out of me. From the outside, it looked like I had life by the tail. Inside was a different story. I was at the point of wanting to escape life altogether.

That was the morning I decided to make some changes. I thought the changes would mostly involve changing my circumstances. I quit my job, ended a 24-year marriage, and moved to a different state. Little did I know that that was only the beginning. The changes I needed to make went far deeper than my surroundings. They involved a part of me that I hardly knew at all. And yet, it was that part of me that held the answers for mending my life and creating the life of my dreams.

It seemed as if this essential part of me were hidden behind closed doors. I didn't know what it looked like or how to access it. I felt very dark, empty, and sad inside. I had tried deadening the inner pain with work, family activities, a busy life-style, and a few drinks every night. Nothing filled the void. My life simply was not working for me. I wasn't willing to live like that anymore. And so, after quitting my job, I devoted my days to understanding how to open those doors. As I did, I discovered something behind them that was incredibly wise and beautiful. I found my soul.

As each door opened, an amazing part of myself was unleashed. The closed doors that were keeping me from living the life of my dreams became the seven portals to my soul. Each one contained its own message for mending my life.

Through the seven portals, I came in touch with that part of me that knows who I really am and why I am here. It knows what I am passionate about. It knows what gives me joy. It helps me to make decisions and live my life with greater ease. My soul has not only helped me mend my life; it has taught me how to really live it.

My life now is everything I had hoped it could be when I began my search seven years ago. It is a life of serenity and peace, of joy and fulfillment, of compassion and unconditional love. It is the life of my dreams. Your life can be the life of your dreams too.

This book contains guidelines for helping you to open the seven portals to your soul as they helped me open mine. It will assist you in accessing that most essential part of your being. It will show you how to mend your life and soar with your soul.

The questionnaire at the end of this chapter will help you determine whether each of the seven portals to your soul is mostly open or mostly closed. You can use it as a preliminary assessment of whether or not you are soaring with your soul.

The Soul's Perspective

I use the word "soul" to describe that part of one's spirit that is most closely connected with the physical body. It resides with the body in the lower dimensions. The soul experiences what we go through in life—our joys, pains, thoughts, and emotions. The soul is a composite of energies, essences, and abilities that make us who we are. It gives us our unique qualities. The soul infuses the body with life. It transforms the body into a human being.

The soul has certain experiences, lessons, and healing to accomplish during its physical life. These, along with other contributions it makes to humanity, Mother Earth, and the Universe, constitute the divine plan for the soul's life. It approaches life as a training ground or school. It finds life to be quite exciting. The soul sees life as a huge challenge and adventure. It is, in some respects, the spiritual equivalent of physically climbing Mount Everest. If we don't get the soul involved, a toll can be taken on our minds, bodies, and emotions. It would be like climbing Mount Everest blind. The soul can see the handholds and footholds, the crevasses and drop-offs.

When we are out of touch with our souls, we depend on our minds and egos to lead the way. They see life from a very limited perspective. The soul sees life from a higher perspective. From the mind's point of view, things can seem very confusing and at odds with one another. When seen through the eyes of the soul, they take on a whole new clarity and understanding. It is similar to the difference in perspectives that one gets when standing on the ground, versus flying in an airplane. One is very narrowly focused; the other is more expansive.

> When we are out of touch with our souls, we depend on our minds and egos to lead the way. They see life from a very limited perspective.

What seems to be an overwhelming mountain, when standing beside it, becomes a captivatingly beautiful and interesting change in the landscape, when viewed from above. What looks to be a place of unending darkness, when standing in it, becomes the outline and shadow of something grand, when seen from above. We are in the shadow of something grand. To see it takes a shift in perspective. This book will help you to make that shift. It will help you to see the grandness of life. It will help you to get in touch with your soul and see life from its perspective.

The soul sometimes forgets what it is to do. It can become stuck in emotions and pain. Another part of our spirits, which I call "The Higher Self", reminds the soul of its mission and helps it to heal and fulfill the divine plan for its life. The Higher Self has direct access to the wisdom of the Universe. It sees life from an even higher perspective than that of the soul.

The Higher Self resides in the higher dimensions. It does not directly experience what we go through in life. It will, however, assist us when asked to do so. It can give us guidance, showing us the next steps to take. It can make things happen more synchronistically. It can give us helpful information, insights, and energy for mending our lives and making them easier. This book will show you how to work with your soul and Higher Self to access their help, wisdom, and energy, and to see life from a higher perspective.

We gain access to the Higher Self through the soul and the heart. The Higher Self is the link between the soul and the "Universe" or "All That Is". I use these terms to describe the oneness of all energy. Some refer to this by such names as The One, Source, God, or Great Spirit. There may be untold other aspects of spirit between the Higher Self and All That Is that serve various other functions. An understanding of these is not pertinent to this book.

"Spirit" is my designation for the unseen force or consciousness that pervades the Universe or All That Is. You may have other ways of naming and describing the various aspects of our spirits. My definitions are not meant to change your language or beliefs. They are simply given to help you understand how the terms are used in this book.

The Seven Portals to the Soul

The seven portals to the soul are the seven major chakras associated with the physical body. Chakras are "energy centers", sometimes described as spinning vortices. They extend all the way through the physical body, the energy fields outside the body, and beyond. Besides the seven major chakras, there are also many minor chakras located at the joints and organs. There are chakras above and below the body as well. An understanding of the chakra system of energy was developed thousands of years ago. Humanity's understanding of it has grown continuously since that time.

The soul makes its connection with the body through the chakras. The chakras are the portals through which the soul materializes into physicality and experiences physical life. They are like transformers that transfer energy between the physical and nonphysical. The more we heal and open our chakras, the more we mend our lives. Through the chakras we gain access to the wisdom, healing energies and life force of our souls, Higher Selves, and All That Is. Closing off our chakras starves us energetically and makes us feel isolated. It is spiritually equivalent to partially cutting off our food, water, and communication lines in the physical. The terms "open" and "closed" are relative. The chakras do not close down completely. Opening them increases their size, energy, effectiveness, and functionality.

Each chakra has one or more functions. These will be discussed in detail in each Portal. The main purpose of the chakras is to help the soul live a fully functioning physical/spiritual life. They help us draw needed people and things into our lives, relate to others, express our individuality, process our emotions, access our guidance, and connect with a higher consciousness. They help us to live life with greater joy and ease.

> The main purpose of the chakras is to help the soul live a fully functioning physical/spiritual life.
>
> When the chakras aren't performing as well as they should, life becomes difficult.

When the chakras aren't performing as well as they should, life becomes difficult. As the chakras close, we lose touch with the aspect of the soul that works through that chakra. We temporarily lose some of our amazing abilities. We begin to feel limited and powerless. We forget who we are.

How well a chakra performs its intended function is based on many things. These will be covered portal by portal. Each chakra is a holding place for certain beliefs, many of which are related to the function of the chakra. Sometimes the beliefs contain misperceptions that limit the functioning and openness of the chakra. For example, if one believes that the world is a place of lack and limitation, then that belief limits the ability of the first chakra to bring abundance into the individual's life. Many self-limiting beliefs such as this one will be addressed throughout this book. Seeing life from the soul's perspective helps to transform these beliefs into those that support a fuller, more joyful, and abundant life.

This Book's Approach to Healing

The purpose of this book is to show how, by healing and opening the chakras, we can heal, or mend, our lives. It adds another perspective to the information already available on the chakras. The chakras are the central point of healing. They are the portals or doorways through which we access the body, mind, emotions, soul, and Higher Self all at the same time.

It is most effective to heal the chakras in order from one to seven. The lower chakras support the functioning of the higher ones, like steps. One wouldn't climb a ladder by starting at the top. One wouldn't build a house from the roof on down. The lower chakras provide a firm foundation upon which to build one's life. The higher chakras take that life into a place of joy and fulfillment.

The opening of each chakra builds upon the healing that was done in the chakras before it. Consequently, the techniques used in the beginning chapters of this book will be drawn upon again in the later chapters. As the higher chakras are addressed, issues in the chakras beneath them may also surface to be healed, and vice versa. The chakras are all connected. Their healing is an integrative process.

Healing ourselves is the most important task we have to do in life. Most of us come into this life with lessons to learn and healing to accomplish. The painful situations we incur remind us of those lessons. The things we find most disturbing can be our greatest teachers. The

> Healing ourselves is the most important task we have to do in life.

exercises and techniques in this book are designed to help you more quickly move through the pain, learn your lessons, and mend your life.

At the beginning of each portal, you will find a figure of a person. There is a spiral on the figure that shows the approximate location of the chakra. Beneath the figure is a chart that contains general information about the chakra. The chart gives a quick overview of the chakra—its name, location and functions. It describes the tendencies of a person when the chakra is open and balanced. It also lists problems and issues that can surface when the chakra is closed and unbalanced. Along with the questionnaire at the end of this chapter, these charts can help you to assess which of your chakras are open or closed.

The traditional color associated with the chakra is also given in the chart. Simultaneously focusing one's awareness on the chakra and its corresponding color can assist with the opening of it. As the chakras open, the overall energy or vibrational level of the body increases. The chakra colors may change or become more pastel to reflect that.

At the bottom of each chart, restoring validations are given. These can help to dissolve one's self-perceived limitations, transform one's destructive beliefs, and increase one's power and effectiveness as spiritual/human beings. They help to open the chakras and bring forth the true essence and power of the soul.

> **Allow your soul to gently guide you into a life that brings you joy and serves your highest good.**

As you read this book, I encourage you to let go of your attachments to whom you think you are, what you think is important, and what you must have. They may no longer be appropriate for you. I made many changes in my life. You may or may not need to do that. Allow your soul to gently guide you into a life that brings you joy and serves your highest good, whatever that may be. It may be different from those around you. Every soul is unique. Each one is here for a specific experience and purpose. That is where we find true happiness and fulfillment.

This book is designed to help you expand your own capabilities to connect with your soul and beyond. There is great wisdom in that part of you. You may wish to come back to this book again and again. Each time you do, your soul and Higher Self will show you something different. The techniques and exercises are powerful tools for healing. They can be referred to often to address any issues and problems that may arise in daily life.

The following questionnaire will help you assess which of your chakras are open or closed. It should help you identify problem areas through checking the appropriate boxes. Is your soul helping you to live the life of your dreams; or is it hiding behind closed doors? It is not a test. There are no wrong answers. But the more items you check in the first column of the questionnaire, the more you can expect this book to help you transform your life.

Are the Portals to Your Soul Open or Closed?

Closed	Open
PORTAL #1	
❑ I don't have a sense of my soul	❑ I feel at one with my soul
❑ I don't have what I need to live	❑ I have abundance
❑ I feel unsafe	❑ I feel protected
❑ I dislike or abuse my body	❑ I love and honor my body
❑ I have frequent mishaps and accidents	❑ I am usually aware of my surroundings
❑ I want to escape	❑ I feel like I belong here

Closed	Open
PORTAL #2	
❑ I am caught up in the drama of my life	❑ I use my life situations to find healing
❑ I blame others for my problems	❑ I see myself in others
❑ I have lost my enthusiasm for life	❑ I embrace my life
❑ I don't feel very creative	❑ I enjoy my creativity
❑ I am out of touch with my sensuality	❑ I relish my sensuality
❑ I have either shut down my emotions or they control my life	❑ I feel the emotions of the moment, accept them, and learn from them
❑ I have unhealthy relationships	❑ The people around me are supportive
❑ I feel lonely and isolated	❑ I feel connected to others
PORTAL #3	
❑ I repeat the same painful situations and relationships over and over again	❑ I learn and evolve from my circumstances and relationships
❑ I usually put myself last	❑ I am good to myself
❑ I often do things out of guilt or obligation	❑ I do what gives me joy
❑ I feel like a victim	❑ I feel powerful
❑ My life is not my own	❑ I take responsibility for my life
PORTAL #4	
❑ I don't know who I am	❑ I know who I am inside
❑ I feel worried, stressed	❑ I am at peace
❑ I often feel put on the defensive	❑ I accept myself for who I am
❑ I run away from my fears	❑ I confront my fears and move through them
❑ My spiritual and physical sides seem disconnected	❑ My physicality and spirituality are integrated

Closed	Open
PORTAL #5	
❑ I feel like I should be doing something different	❑ I feel good about the direction of my life
❑ I tell people what they want to hear	❑ I speak my truth
❑ I try to be what others want me to be	❑ I am true to myself
❑ I feel the need to impress others	❑ I do things for my own satisfaction
❑ I don't like what I do daily	❑ I love my life
❑ I am afraid of being different from others	❑ I enjoy my uniqueness
PORTAL #6	
❑ My life is chaotic	❑ My life is in balance
❑ My life feels stifled and limited	❑ My life is full of possibilities
❑ I don't have a vision for my life	❑ I have a wonderful vision for my life
❑ I seem to sabotage my dreams	❑ My life is the life of my dreams
❑ There are parts of me that feel like total opposites	❑ All parts of me work together in harmony
❑ I feel scattered and incomplete	❑ I feel whole and integrated
PORTAL #7	
❑ I have trouble making decisions	❑ I make decisions that support my highest good
❑ I feel pulled in many different directions at the same time	❑ I feel unified in my intent
❑ There is constant chatter in my mind	❑ My mind is usually clear and calm
❑ I depend on others to tell me what to do	❑ I make my own choices
❑ My life is hard	❑ My life flows with ease

How did you do? Don't be alarmed if most, or even all, of your checks ended up in the first column. That is where most of mine were seven years ago. But that has completely changed for me, and it can change for you too. It takes patience, diligence, and the willingness to approach your life from a different perspective—the perspective of your soul.

As you open each of the seven portals to your soul, you will discover a greater freedom. Whole new vistas will open up before you. You will connect with that very powerful part of yourself that will help you to mend your life and create the life of your dreams. Have fun! Soar! Flying isn't just for angels anymore.

As you open the first chakra, you will bring your soul more fully into your body to connect with the planet that supports your life.

That is the first and most essential step to mending your life and soaring with your soul.

welcome to

THE FIRST PORTAL

to your soul…

The First Portal

Name	First or Root Chakra
Location	Base of spine and perineum
Traditional Color	Red
Functions	• Anchors the soul into the body and to the earth • Attracts what is needed to live
Balanced Tendencies	Sense of groundedness, belonging, safety, protection, abundance; physical needs supplied; general well-being; physical strength; acceptance and appreciation of the body
Unbalanced Tendencies	Ungroundedness; prone to accidents; lack of physical support; self-abuse; lack of body awareness; judgments regarding the body's beauty; lack of concern for the earth
Physical Problems	Pain in tailbone and sacrum, sciatica, varicose veins, rectal tumors, leg and foot disorders
Mental and Emotional Issues	Feels unsafe and vulnerable; survival and money fears; hypochondria; greed; paranoia; escapism; abuse or disapproval of the body
Restoring Validations	I am safe. I belong here. My life is important. There is enough for all. The earth and the Universe support me. My body is a beautiful and worthy creation.

PORTAL #1

Reconnect With Your Soul by Staying Grounded

Do you remember times when you felt totally "in your body"—those moments when it felt really good to be alive? Maybe you felt that way while walking in the woods or sitting by a beautiful lake, feeling very peaceful and connected to the nature around you. Or maybe it happened during a relaxing massage, or while soaking in the bath or hot tub, or during a good workout. Or perhaps it was when you were completely focused on what you were doing at the time, and that concentrated attention made you feel more alive, more "with it", more conscious of your surroundings, and more aware of every sensation. The feelings just described are what it is like to be fully grounded—to be "down to earth", so to speak, when the body is at one with the soul, and fully connected to Mother Earth.

On the other hand, do you also recall times when you felt very disconnected from your body? Maybe it was when you were so tired, from burning the candle at both ends, that you just went through the motions of your daily routine—feeling more like a robot than a human being. Or maybe it was during a particularly stressful or painful time of your life, when anxiety or depression caused you to disconnect from your surroundings. Or maybe it happened while you were still sedated following surgery, or under the influence of drugs or too much alcohol. This is what it is like to be ungrounded. It happens when the body and soul are not completely merged with one another and the earth. It gives one the feeling of being out of control, disconnected, and removed from reality.

Most people have times of being more grounded, or less grounded, depending upon what is going on in their lives. The examples above depict opposite ends of the spectrum. There is a great deal that happens in between, most of which we rarely pay much attention to. But if we did, we would understand why sometimes we feel more vibrant, alive, and supported than we do at other times.

> It is the job of the first chakra to bring the soul into the body.
>
> It is imperative to our health, abundance, well being, and spiritual evolution, to keep this portal open.

It is the job of the first chakra to bring the soul into the body. This is the portal through which the soul grounds and supports itself on the physical plane. The further closed this portal becomes, the more difficult it is for the individual to carry on an abundant and pleasurable life. The soul does not receive the full benefit of living this life, either. It can not "carry the lessons home" because it is disconnected from the body that is experiencing them.

As you read on, you will see why it is imperative to our health, abundance, and well being as humans, as well as to our spiritual evolution, to keep this portal open. You will learn how to open the first portal by becoming grounded. You will learn how to recognize and resolve the issues that prevent you from staying grounded—the issues that keep this chakra closed. As you open the first chakra, you will bring your soul more fully into your body to connect with the planet that supports your life. That is the first and most essential step toward mending your life and soaring with your soul.

The Importance of Being Grounded

We are spiritual beings living a physical life. When we are grounded, we bring more of our spiritual self into our physical self. There are many benefits to doing this. These include being better able to access our inner guidance, being protected, making better use of the energy that is available to us, and drawing to us all that we need to live a comfortable life on the physical plane. These shall be discussed one by one.

Guidance

The first benefit to being grounded is that it gives us the ability to connect with that part of us that knows why we are here. Our true wisdom comes through the soul. It is not in our intellect, as the ego would have us believe. Living one's physical life without the input of one's soul is like living it in the dark. The soul illuminates life. It guides us through life to draw to us the experiences for which it has come.

Later in this book, you will learn how to access your guidance. Grounding is an essential part of receiving guidance, for it helps to ensure that what is received is from one's own soul and Higher Self, and not from the ego or something else. Have you been wondering what your life is all about? Does it seem to lack meaning for you? Becoming grounded is the first step to discovering who you are and why you are here.

Protection

Being protected is another benefit of being grounded. When we are grounded, we are safer physically. We are less accident-prone. We are more aware of our surroundings, because our bodies are connected to the earth. Before I learned how to ground myself, I was constantly tripping over things—cracks in the sidewalk, tree roots and rocks on forested trails, stairs, and even my own feet. On one camping excursion we took with my son's youth group, one of his friends asked him if I were always that clumsy. Since I've become grounded, I don't trip anymore. I can hike through the woods without engaging a single tree root. I can't remember the last time I fell, or banged my head, and I rarely bump into things.

Grounding connects us to the nature kingdom. We have a high deer population where I live. Every time I drive, I see one or two deer lying by the side of the road, having jumped in front of a car or truck during the night. Recently I have noticed quite a few deer standing by the side of the road as I pass at night. But they do not run in front of my car. I believe that they sense my presence because I am grounded. When the soul is truly grounded in the body, very few, if any, accidents happen.

When the soul is truly grounded in the body, very few, if any, accidents happen.

Our souls protect us in other ways too. When they are present in our bodies, we are far less susceptible to discordant energies. When the soul is not fully present, we are left open to all kinds of other energies that we may not care to experience, including harmful energies from other people, or even possession by other spirits. The void will somehow be filled. If it is not filled with our own soul, something else will take its place.

Energy

Grounding also helps us to hold a higher vibration in our bodies, and to do it with greater ease. Increasing our body's vibration facilitates our healing in many ways. It can stimulate the cells to heal faster by giving them more energy. It can aid the unblocking of emotional imbalances and areas of stuck energy caused by past emotional, physical, and mental trauma. It can help us to become aware of, and change, negative mental programming that makes us feel small, unworthy, and limited. If we are not grounded, it is very difficult to raise our vibration. The energy has nowhere to go. It doesn't flow. It is like putting water into a pinched off garden hose.

Trying to increase one's vibration without being grounded can make one uncomfortable and even more ungrounded. I had that experience before I understood the importance of being grounded. A friend and I took a beginning level Reiki class. In Reiki, an energy practitioner acts as a transmitter of the life force energy that comes from the Universe. It is one way of increasing the body's vibration.

The night after the first class, my friend was attempting to ease the aching in my tired legs by doing a typical handhold on the occipital area at the back of my head. The aching became worse instead of better, and I had to ask him to stop. The energy that was stuck in my legs was acting much like a restricted garden hose, causing the incoming energy to build up further in my legs. If I had grounded myself first, or if he had begun by holding my feet and helping me to ground, it would have been much more effective in unblocking the stuck, sluggish, energy that was causing the aching.

We get energy from the Universe all the time, not just when we receive energy work through someone else. Some of it comes from the sun, but there are also other sources. At this time, the vibration of the earth is increasing at a very rapid rate. If one is not grounded, the increase in energy will not feel very good. There may be more mood swings, more anger and anxiety, more mental turmoil, and more aches, pain, and disease, in the areas that are already burdened or stuck. One may feel very tired and more ungrounded than ever. It sometimes feels like the flu. Perhaps you have felt some of these symptoms yourself, and chalked it up to stress or old age.

It is not just old age! You will find that the more you are able to stay grounded, and every day open up the areas where energy is stuck, the more you will begin to reverse these symptoms. The earth holds all the vibrations that we need for healing—vibrations like hope, compassion, forgiveness, unconditional love, and the vibrations used to balance the light and dark energies into wholeness. Your grounding cord is the conduit through which these vibrations are accessed. We will frequently use these healing vibrations from the earth, in the exercises throughout the book. As you do these exercises, your vibration will increase. You will experience an increase in energy, vitality, and well-being, a renewed zest for life, and a more youthful countenance.

> The earth's healing vibrations are accessed through your grounding cord.

Survival

Grounding to the earth is necessary for our survival and to manifest our dreams. The earth works with us like an amplifier to disperse our intentions and vibrations so that the circumstances and people needed to help us live our lives and manifest our dreams can be drawn to us. We do this through the first chakra. It is done by thought, intention, and positive emotion.

Imagine your aura, or energy field, expanding out as far as possible. Then place your intentions and desires in your energy field. Give your intentions a boost by putting some emotional energy behind them. Intend that whatever is needed to fulfill these intentions, desires, and dreams be drawn to you and funneled up through the portal of the first chakra.

The graphic below may help you visualize how this is done. Just be sure that what you ask for is *really* what you want!

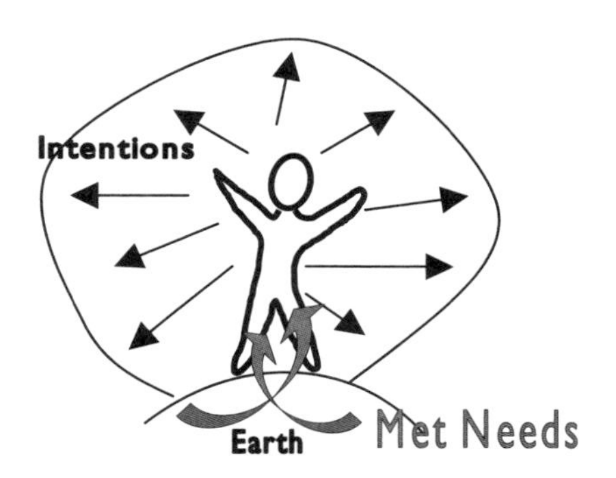

I consult my soul and Higher Self to make sure it is for my best and highest good and the good of all. Maintaining a strong, clear vision of your wants and needs is important.

My partner and I enjoy playing pool. He had been envisioning having a pool table in the basement of our home. He saw in his mind's eye a beautiful, 4' X 8' table. (The larger regulation size would have been too big for the space). He wanted one made of slate, rather than plywood. Tables like that sell for at least $3000 new. Ron had been holding this vision loosely for years. He began to hold the vision daily, and with stronger intensity. About a month after Ron did this, his boss asked him if he would like to have their pool table. They were moving and didn't want to take it with them. The table was a 4' X 8' slate table in excellent condition. Even the felt was like new. It was a beautiful design – the top of the line when it was purchased. My partner's vision is now sitting in our basement – a physical reality.

It is important not to worry about how your vision will manifest. Don't worry about how much it will cost. Don't even think about how you will pay for it. Just hold the vision.

We needed new kitchen appliances. The refrigerator, stove, and dishwasher were all 25 years old – when harvest gold was all the rage. The dishwasher was so loud that we couldn't talk on the kitchen phone when it was running. We had to wash all the food off the dirty dishes before washing them in the dishwasher. Otherwise they would come out with food encrusted on them. The dishwasher was also beginning to leak. I envisioned a quiet dishwasher that would make the dirtiest dishes sparkle. It would wash anything from crystal to roasting pans. The pilot lights on the stove wouldn't stay lit. The oven had to be cleaned manually. I envisioned a large self-clean oven and dependable gas burners. The refrigerator/freezer worked well, but never seemed to have enough room in it. I envisioned having a larger refrigerator in the kitchen, and putting the old one in the garage.

I held this vision loosely for about a year. At that time the appliances began to act up worse than ever. I strengthened the intensity of my vision. Every time I walked into the kitchen, I saw the brand new appliances that I have described sitting where the old ones were. They were quiet, worked beautifully, and were in a lovely, light bisque color. About two months later, money for the appliances became available through some unusual circumstances. We now have my vision sitting in our kitchen as a physical reality.

Allow the vision to be manifested in whatever way it will. I would not have imagined the money for the appliances to become available in the way that it did. I could have imagined it to become available in various other ways. Putting a limitation like that on the vision increases the time it takes to bring the vision into reality. It decreases the flexibility of the Universe to make it happen.

Staying grounded helps to make our lives easier and more productive. It is an essential element of drawing to us the things we need to live. It keeps us safe. It gives us access to the wisdom of our souls and the vibrations of the earth. It helps us to live the lives we are meant to live. It is necessary for our sustenance, healing, and evolution.

You have seen the importance of staying grounded. You may be wondering how to tell whether or not you are grounded. It is not too difficult, for there are telltale signs. The more ungrounded one is, the more obvious are the signs.

What It Is Like To Be Grounded or Ungrounded

There is a continuum of groundedness. The further down in the body the soul is able to go, the more grounded it is. The higher it hovers in the body, the less grounded it is. There are certain telltale signs that indicate how grounded or ungrounded a person is. These can differ from one person to the next, depending upon what is causing the first chakra to shut down.

Fully Grounded

There are various degrees of groundedness. When one is fully grounded, the soul encompasses the whole body, all the way down to the toes, and is connected to the center of the earth. There is a feeling of protection, stability, abundance, support, well-being, and strength.

Slightly Ungrounded

Being slightly ungrounded means that the soul is no longer fully connected to the earth and thus does not encompass the lower part of the body. It may go only as far as the knees, for example, or slightly higher than that. People can very easily live out their lives in this condition. They can function fairly "normally", but they are probably prone to minor accidents—tripping, stubbing their toes, and bumping into things. They may have problems with their feet, ankles, or knees, such as aches, pains, sprains, or broken bones. They may have an occasional major accident. There may be some difficulty accessing their guidance. They may wish they had more enthusiasm for life, feel as if they don't belong here, or feel unsupported on the physical plane.

Moderately Ungrounded

People who are moderately ungrounded may have those problems too, plus some others. They may become nauseous or light-headed, depending upon how high their soul is hovering above the ground. It may go down only as far as the head or chest, for example. They are not very aware of their surroundings, feel rather unstable, and shouldn't drive. The chances for getting into an accident are high. They may be quite prone to attracting energies that are not theirs, which can result in confusion, paranoia, misdirection, anxiety, fear, or mood swings. They may have a strong disregard for the earth or their own bodies.

Severely Ungrounded

People who are severely ungrounded may be zombie-like or drift in and out of consciousness. It may be difficult or impossible for them to walk or function on the physical plane because they are so unaware of what is going on and have little control of their bodies. Their souls must be brought back into their bodies so that they don't become inhabited by another spirit or cross the line between this life and the next.

One may wonder why people become ungrounded, when grounding is such a desirable and helpful state in which to be. What causes some to be more or less grounded than others?

The Causes of Ungroundedness

There are a myriad of circumstances, events, and our reactions to them that can cause the first chakra to close and unground the soul. Most of them have something to do with a desire to escape painful feelings or situations, not wanting to participate fully in this physical life, or not wanting the soul to be in charge (which can be a conscious or unconscious choice).

All of these are understandable reactions to this physical life, and the pains we have endured. The experience of ungroundedness has served us in its own way, deadening the pain in our lives. But now it is time to heal the pain and to stay grounded, so the soul can truly do its work. Staying grounded is the first step toward mending our lives. Some of the causes of ungroundedness are described below.

Holding the Breath

When we are in situations that are highly emotional, stressful, or fearful, we tend to hold our breath. Unconsciously, we are trying to escape the situation, or keep from feeling it. But holding our breath ungrounds us, makes us even more tense, and diverts the pain to our cells, where the memory of it is held. Storing pain of any sort in our cells closes down our chakras. So each time we hold our breath to avoid pain, we close our first chakra a little more.

Breathing deeply helps to bring the soul into the body, allowing us to let go of the pain and relax. People who take full breaths usually find it easier to stay grounded than those who take shallow breaths. Conscious breathing helps us to stay in the present. Holding our breath takes us out of the present moment. It is a form of escape.

Living in Fantasy

Living in fantasy is also a form of escape. It takes us out of the present and ungrounds us. Most of us live in fantasy to some degree, and we don't even know it. Fantasy is anything in one's life that is not in alignment with the soul, or that takes one out of the present moment. It can be an intentional escape from life or an unconscious one. Both are ungrounding. One way to enter into fantasy is to dwell on the past or to live for

> Fantasy is anything in one's life that is not in alignment with the soul, or that takes one out of the present moment.

the future. The soul lives in the present moment. That is why focusing on what we are doing, and experiencing the sensations of the moment, is so grounding.

Another way that we enter into fantasy is by allowing the ego to take charge of our lives. That can happen when we deny our spiritual side, refuse to follow the promptings of the soul, or lose touch with the soul. The ego plays an important role in this life—to get things done on the physical plane. Its purpose is to be a support to the soul. It helps us to manifest the soul's visions here on earth. When we lose touch with the soul, we rely on the ego to direct us. When it does, we can very easily be led down the wrong path. We end up living in fantasy and out of alignment with the true purposes and desires of the soul. That can be very ungrounding and also very stressful. The difference between living from the soul and living in fantasy will be discussed in detail in Portal #7.

Addictions

Addictions are another form of escape—drinking to dull the pain of life, doing drugs, sitting in front of the TV or doing computer games for hours on end, etc. All of these can be ungrounding. Our intention is the key. For example, if the intention of drinking alcohol is to celebrate life or to enhance one's enjoyment of it—like a good glass of wine with dinner—then one can stay grounded. If the intention is to binge drink to escape one's problems, or to drink until the stress of the day is forgotten, then there is a good chance that it will be ungrounding.

Pain

Intense physical, mental, or emotional pain can cause ungroundedness. It is the spiritual equivalent of going into shock. Serious injuries, abuse, rape, torture, or mind-control can cause one to become ungrounded and also to go into fantasy to avoid acknowledging or remembering the pain of the situation. It is a protective mechanism. Breathing through these situations and consciously dealing with them afterwards can prevent them from becoming stuck in the cells.

Most, if not all, of us have past experiences, we have not cared to acknowledge or deal with, that have become stuck in our cellular structure. Unresolved issues such as these can unground us and close our chakras. They are usually the root cause of addiction and other harmful behaviors. When we heal our past, it is much easier to keep our chakras open and to stay grounded. The exercises in this book will help you to uncover and heal issues from your past.

As an intuitive and massage therapist, I have seen people become moderately to severely ungrounded, during energy work or healing sessions, as they unconsciously resist the healing of the issues that have surfaced. I begin my sessions by helping my clients to ground. Any issues that might prevent them from grounding tend to surface immediately. When these issues are dealt with first, the healing session is much more productive. The soul is then present to access the wisdom, love, and healing vibrations of the Higher Self and the earth. The commitment of the soul and Higher Self to heal usually overcomes the resistance of the mind.

The next few points have to do with parts of ourselves that many don't recognize or hardly notice—our energy fields—which are in and around our physical bodies. Our energy fields are just as much a part of us as our physical bodies, and affect our ability to ground. They contain a great deal of information, although we aren't usually aware of it on a conscious level.

Missing Information

One of the pieces of information that is contained in our energy fields is how to stay grounded. For one reason or another, in some people, this information is missing. If, after you do the grounding exercise found later in this chapter, you still aren't able to stay grounded, you might want to call back this information. As you fall asleep at night, intend that your information for grounding be given to you. It will go into your unconscious; therefore, it won't be something that you "remember" on the conscious level. Our souls can do a tremendous amount of work while we sleep, especially when we set the intention for it just prior to dozing off.

Missing Gridwork

There is an energy body, called the etheric body, which lies just outside the physical body. It contains information on how the physical body is constructed. The etheric body is made up of many interlocking gridlines of moving energy. They are similar to the meridians in the physical body that the acupuncturists use, but they are much closer together. If part of the etheric gridwork is damaged or missing, that part of the physical body will most likely become diseased or damaged as well, over time. The chakra in that area of the body will also not function as well. Part of the etheric gridwork supports our grounding. If the gridwork is missing in the lower legs, it is very difficult to ground. The gridwork must be called back and, with it, the gridwork for grounding. This can be done even if one has lost his or her legs.

> If part of the etheric gridwork is damaged or missing, that part of the physical body will most likely become diseased or damaged as well, over time.

I have "seen", through my intuitive knowing, many people who are walking around with their gridwork missing from the knees on down. There is not much energy there, and they have problems grounding. Most have also experienced some kind of physical difficulty in that area—knee or ankle pain, broken leg or ankle bones, edema, etc. Oftentimes this is related to issues of not feeling safe, supported, or taken care of. It is similar to the feeling of having "the rug pulled out from under you". One may be fearful of losing everything he or she has, or of not having enough. Healing these fears and calling back the gridwork will help the individual to ground, and may also help to resolve the physical problems in the lower legs. Fear can close down the chakras. You will be shown how to heal your fears further along in this book.

Fear can close down the chakras. You will be shown how to heal your fears further along in this book.

Wrong Energy Signature

Sometimes the energies we carry in and around our bodies can unground the soul, especially when they are not in alignment with the soul and body.

There is one energy in particular that should be given close consideration; that is the energy of one's gender. This energy begins above the top of the head, runs down through the body, and into the earth—if it is in alignment with the gender of the body. As it does so, it draws the soul down into the body. For women, the energy signature is a series of widely curved

The energy signature for one's gender begins above the top of the head, runs down through the body, and into the earth. It grounds the soul into the body.

parallel waves. For men, it is a series of narrowly curved waves. The following diagram depicts the energy signatures of both men and women.

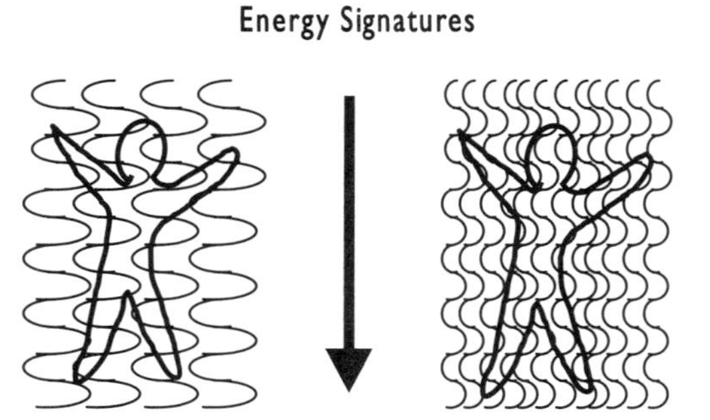

If women run the male energy configuration, or if men run the female energy signature, it sets up a reverse polarity in the body similar to the repulsion that happens when like poles of two magnets are brought together. The energy runs up instead of down, drawing the soul to the upper part of the body. This can happen when there are unresolved issues of sexuality—when the masculine and feminine sides of oneself have not been integrated and are in competition with one another. It does not have anything to do with one's sexual orientation.

Each gender's energy signature has a side that is more masculine and a side that is more feminine. There is a lot of leeway. Just because a girl is a "Tom Boy" or a man is effeminate, does not necessarily mean they are running the wrong energy signature.

I have seen many clients who have had difficulty staying grounded because they have unresolved issues surrounding the integration of their own masculine and feminine sides. This usually manifests itself in outward competition between the sexes or within their own sex. When these are forgiven and resolved, the individuals are able to run the energy signature appropriate to their gender, and stay grounded.

If you suspect that you might be running the wrong energy signature, then ask your soul to reveal to you what the issues are so that you can heal them. You will learn how to do that in Portal #6. If your intent is to stay grounded, you will eventually be given the information and the healing you need for it to happen. Let's see how grounding occurs.

How to Ground Yourself

If you know that you tend to be ungrounded, it is important to ground yourself often. I recommend grounding when going to sleep, upon waking up, when driving (ground the vehicle too) and when under stress or not feeling quite right. Eventually, grounding becomes automatic, as we resolve the issues that cause us to be ungrounded. Even so, I always check to make sure I am grounded before I pray, meditate, ask for guidance, or do any kind of healing work. It helps to put me in touch with my soul and Higher Self, protects me, and keeps the wisdom and energy of the Universe flowing through me. You will be asked to ground yourself when you do the exercises in this book.

There are many things we can do to help us stay grounded. Breathing is one of them, as we have noted. Eating is another. Many find protein and chocolate to be particularly grounding. Being in nature is another good way to ground—going for walks in the woods, lying on the grass, or hugging a tree. Animals are part of the nature kingdom too. Having a pet can be grounding.

Since our legs are important vehicles for our grounding, we must keep the energy moving in them. There are minor chakras in the feet that assist with grounding and the movement of our energy. Walking, dancing, or stamping one's feet can open these chakras.

Our intention to ground to the center of the earth is the most important aspect of grounding. Grounding from the base of the spine (the center of the first chakra), and the bottoms of the feet, are most effective. Imagine beams of light energy connecting your tailbone and feet to the earth as you walk. We used to envision roots extending into the earth from the bottoms of our feet. But the energies are much lighter now, and they are changing very fast. The fluidity of light is a more appropriate image to elicit at this time. Imagine the connection being renewed and revitalized with every step. The energies are changing that fast.

Our intention to ground to the center of the earth is the most important aspect of grounding.

Grounding can be done no matter what you are doing—talking with friends, driving the car, doing your daily routine, or meditating. The first few times you do it, however, it is strongly suggested that you get into a quiet space by yourself in order to focus better as you practice the visualizations. You can do this standing up, sitting, or lying down. You can use the grounding exercise to help you set your intention. When you have become familiar with it, it will take only a few seconds to ground yourself.

When you are grounded, you should feel more alert and very present in your body, all the way down to your toes. You should feel more stable in your stance, safe, and connected to the earth. Your senses may be heightened. You may even feel more energy in your body, or tingling in your feet or legs, depending upon how sensitive you are to energy. Get to know how it feels to you to be grounded. And ground yourself often.

Exercise – Grounding Yourself

1. *Take several deep, cleansing breaths*
2. *Imagine an invisible beam of light that extends from the base of your spine all the way to the center of the earth. This is your main "grounding cord". You may make it as thick as you like, even ten feet in diameter. Set the intention for the energy to keep moving down into the earth from your body through this grounding cord. It must never be stagnant.*
3. *Imagine two more beams of light, coming up from the center of the earth and connecting to the bottoms of your feet. Ask your Higher Self to bring up from the earth whatever vibrations you are in need of in this moment, especially those that will remove or balance any obstacles to your being grounded. The energy in these two grounding cords runs from the center of the earth to your body, through your feet.*
4. *Continue to bring up the earth vibrations through the bottoms of your feet, all throughout your body. Imagine them coming up your calves, knees, thighs, and hips. Intend that some of the energy spills over into the grounding cord that goes down from the base of your spine, keeping the energy of the grounding cord moving and releasing any energies into the earth that are stuck and no longer serve your highest good. Intend that the rest of the earth energies go up your torso, along your spine, out the top of your head, and spill out over the sides of your body. They wash your auric field (the energy field outside your body) as they descend down the outside of your body back into the earth. Keep these vibrations flowing, as if you are in a steady stream of fluid light that constantly cleanses, refreshes, heals, and rejuvenates.*
5. *Intend that the energy signature for your gender run down through your body, grounding your soul fully in your body and into the earth. Use the earth vibrations to dissolve, balance, or remove anything that is keeping you from being fully grounded.*

Sometimes, even though we have set our intention to ground, and done everything we can think of to stay grounded, we may still have difficulty grounding. When this happens, it usually means we have run up against something that is blocking our grounding. It may be one of those old issues from the past that was mentioned earlier. In the next portal, you will learn how to use the people and circumstances in your life to uncover these blocks and reflect upon the issues that are causing them. You will learn how to become the observer of your life, tapping into the wisdom of your soul. This will help you to stay grounded. It is also paramount to mending anything in your life that is causing it to be a struggle.

> When the second portal to the soul is open, working, and balanced, we savor the experience of life...living it with gusto.

welcome to

THE SECOND PORTAL

to your soul…

The Second Portal

Name	Second or Navel Chakra
Location	2-3 inches below navel, next to spleen
Traditional Color	Orange
Functions	• Connects the soul with the substance of life sensually, sexually, and emotionally • Self-discovery and creativity
Balanced Tendencies	Verve for life; self-awareness; honoring relationships; healthy expression of emotions, sexuality, and sensuality; creative; trusting
Unbalanced Tendencies	Melodramatic; out of touch; tumultuous relationships; betrayal; blame; distrust; resentment; denial of or preoccupation with physical or sensual pleasure; lack of creativity
Physical Problems	Low back, hip, or pelvic pain; ob/gyn problems; unbalanced libido; impotence; problems with large intestine, urinary tract, appendix, spleen
Mental and Emotional Issues	Sexual or emotional abuse and disorders; social fears; unhealthy relationships; controlled by the emotions or emotional suppression; withdrawal; loneliness; obsessive/compulsive disorders
Restoring Validations	I enjoy my body and my life. I delight in my creativity. I feel my emotions. I embrace my sexuality. I relish my sensuality. I honor my relationships.

PORTAL #2

Dispel the Drama by Becoming the Observer

"All the world's a stage,
And all the men and women merely players:
They have their exits and their entrances;
And one man in his time plays many parts."
—William Shakespeare, *As You Like It*

Shakespeare had the right idea. The world is indeed a stage. Our lives are one continuous drama—sometimes comedy and sometimes tragedy. The main acts open and close. People come in and out. And various themes weave their way through the many scenes of our lives.

Here on earth, our souls assume a multitude of roles to give us experiences that we wouldn't otherwise have outside of this dimension. We assemble a physical body (the costume), a set of circumstances (the stage), physical supports (props), and other people (characters) to play out one episode after another (scenes). Each episode and relationship is provided to teach us important lessons. They give us opportunities to see who we are in a particular situation, discover our prevailing thoughts and behaviors, learn about our gifts and self-imposed limitations, and enhance our awareness of life in this dimension. What a wonderful gift our souls have been given, to try things on this way, and experience them!

Yet, sometimes we get so caught up in the drama, we forget to look beneath it to discover who we really are. We focus on the props, the scenery, the costumes, and the backdrops, and then wonder why the meaning of the script and the richness of our character have eluded us. We learn very few lessons—and those very slowly—as a result.

Sometimes we get so caught up in the drama, we forget to look beneath it to discover who we really are.

We force our souls to replay the same dramas over and over again, much like the movie "Groundhog Day", until we discover the meaning of the script. When we miss it the first time, a similar scene is created in a different city, a new workplace, or with the next lover, to teach us the lesson. Our souls are very patient and creative. They devise one opportunity after another to awaken us to ourselves and to teach us the lessons that are important for our evolution. But the scenarios they create are not always situations we desire to experience multiple times!

Perhaps you or someone you know has gone from one romantic relationship to another, sabotaging each one in a similar way. Or maybe the same problems surface again and again with people at work—one job after another. Or maybe there is a recurrent feeling of being left out, shunned, or isolated. These are all signs that the second portal to the soul is not functioning as well as it could.

The second chakra is the portal through which our souls connect with the substance of life. It is through this portal that we experience the pleasures and pains of our physicality. This is where we come in touch with our sensuality, our sexuality, our emotional connectedness with others, and our environment. How we feel about and respond to the people, pleasures, and pains in our lives tells us a lot about ourselves. It is a good indication of whether this portal is open or closed. Learning how to become the observer in our life's situations is the first step toward knowing ourselves and mending the issues that keep us from embracing and enjoying life.

> **Learning how to become the observer is the first step toward knowing ourselves.**

When this portal is open, working, and balanced, we live life with gusto. We connect with our surroundings, explore our creativity, relish our sensuality, and enjoy our sexuality. We acknowledge and appreciate each of our relationships as opportunities for life enrichment, emotional connection, self-awareness, healing, and growth. Through this open portal, we savor the experience of life.

When the second portal is closed and unbalanced, life is quite a different story. The gusto is gone. Taking its place is a lackluster existence obscured by fear, resentment, and denial. Emotional connections are severed as relationships are compromised. Sensuality is suppressed; sexuality is censored; and creativity is criticized. The substance of life is kept at a distance, causing the passion for life to wane.

This is the portal through which our souls experience themselves on the physical plane. We can choose to enjoy the experience. Or we can refuse to participate, shutting the world and others out, denying ourselves the tantalizing adventure of self-discovery.

Jack Nicholson's character, Melvin Udall, in the movie *As Good As It Gets* was the perfect example of an individual with a closed second chakra that began to open. The crabby, reclusive writer found little enjoyment in life until he allowed himself to connect with it. His connection began with Verdall, the little dog, and blossomed into a caring relationship with Carol, the waitress, and Simon, the artist. As he opened himself up to a fuller expression of his emotions and sensuality, he also began to heal the obsessive/compulsive behaviors that separated him from others and the world around him.

Most of us have not carried things to that extreme. But in hundreds of other ways, we have held back on the very things that could make our lives so much richer. We have been too busy to spend time with those we love. We have put limitations on our ability to be intimate. We have forgotten to savor the taste of fine food, the emotional depth of great poetry, or the beauty of a leisurely walk in the woods. Our souls need to experience these things. They want to heal anything that prevents us from fully entering into the experience of this life.

> Jack Nicholson's character, Melvin Udall, in the movie *As Good As It Gets* was the perfect example of an individual with a closed second chakra that began to open.

We can be positively sure that, just like Melvin, our souls will continue to bring people and circumstances into our lives that will help us to heal. The people may annoy us. The circumstances may feel painful. We may be tempted to push them away or to block them out. But they have something to teach us about ourselves. It behooves us to pay attention to them.

How do we become aware of the lessons these people and circumstances are teaching us? How do we stop the endless cycle of pain of our own personal "Groundhog Day"? How do we begin to open our second chakras to relate more deeply to others, get back in touch with our sensuality, and enjoy the pleasures of our physicality? We begin by becoming the observer of our lives. Being willing to take a look at, and reflect upon, how we express ourselves and respond to each situation begins to open up this vibrant portal to our souls.

In this chapter, you will be given an opportunity to increase your powers of self- observation. You will learn how to step back and become the audience of your life, while still participating fully in it. You will learn how to take stock of your thoughts, emotions, reactions, and behaviors to bring more healing, enjoyment, appreciation, and gusto to your life and relationships.

Being the Observer

What does it mean to be the observer? How is it done? What is the result? The observer looks inward for the reasons behind life's struggles. The first requirement of the observer is to take responsibility for one's own life situations, and one's reactions to them, no matter what they are. The observer sets the intention to learn from life's experiences, rather than blaming others for them. Observers use the mirror of the people, events, and circumstances around them, to bring to their conscious awareness something that is going on subconsciously or unconsciously within themselves.

The observer looks inward for the reasons behind life's struggles.

Taking on the role of observer gives the soul permission to bring forth information about oneself that might otherwise be missed. The observer asks for this information to be revealed, and then remains open to receiving it in any number of ways. It can come as a thought, or through writing or journaling, or simply through a feeling or awareness. It can come through a book, conversation, tape, or happenstance.

Looking inward can be done alone or with another person. I oftentimes find that talking with a friend about what I have been experiencing brings more clarity to the situation. Ideas and insights frequently pour forth unimpeded when we share compassion and acceptance for one another. We aren't necessarily asking the other for answers; we are simply combining our energies to see more clearly what is behind the drama we have created.

What does observation do for us? It helps us to expand our awareness, listen to our soul, and heal the wounds that have caused us to disconnect from others and our environment. It helps us to learn about the deep parts of ourselves that aren't obvious on the surface. It helps us to make the most of every situation in which we find ourselves. Life becomes a very rich cornucopia of nourishing lessons and information, when we become the observer of it.

The people that share the stage of our lives are our most significant teachers. We have a tendency to want to retreat from those we find frustrating. But they are oftentimes the ones that can teach us the most about ourselves. By becoming the observer, we can turn the frustrating drama, and its associated pain, into healing.

The people that share the stage of our lives are our most significant teachers.

Projection: The One-Way Mirror

Have you ever noticed that people tend to point out the traits of others that they themselves have? Kind people notice the kindnesses of others. Messy people call attention to the disorganization of those around them. Verbose people are critical of those who talk a lot. This is called projection.

Projection happens when a mannerism, behavior, trait, emotion, or reaction of another person pushes a button of familiarity within us. The button is usually hidden deep inside our subconscious or unconscious self. On the surface there may be a strong emotional reaction, such as anger, resentment, or disdain. Beneath the surface lies the very same trait, hidden from our view under a veil of denial.

We oftentimes criticize the object of our projection, not realizing that we are criticizing the same thing within ourselves. It is similar to looking through a one-way mirror at others, unable to see the reflection of ourselves. Native elder Kendall Rice (Ojibway Potowotome, Minneapolis, MN) says, "Whenever you point a finger at someone else, remember there are three fingers pointing back at you." Jesus, according to Matthew[1], warned, "Judge not, that you be not judged".

Holding up the Mirror

When we turn the one-way mirror around, the people around us become mirrors for us. What we see in them is a reflection of something within us. It is helpful to think of the people around us as aspects of ourselves. The traits we share with them are usually the things about them that we notice the most. For example:

> When we turn the one-way mirror around, the people around us become mirrors for us. What we see in them is a reflection of something within us.

If Elizabeth appreciates Alice for her compassionate nature, it is a good indication that Elizabeth also has the capacity to be compassionate. Elizabeth may or may not be aware of or appreciate her own ability to be compassionate. That is the benefit of holding up the mirror - to learn more about ourselves.

Likewise, if Elizabeth judges Audrey for the way she constantly places herself at the center of attention, it is likely that Elizabeth secretly desires to hold that place of attention herself. She may not even realize it. In fact, she may have

[1] Matt. 7:1, *The Holy Bible*. (R.S.V.)

unconsciously submerged that desire because she thought it inappropriate or "bad", or was afraid of it.

Elizabeth may see herself as humble or shy, hiding in the background. If she continues to project her disapproval onto others who are at the center of attention, Elizabeth may never come to realize that, at some level, she shares this ability with them.

Elizabeth's soul may, in fact, be calling her to do something where she *is* the center of attention—do public speaking, for example. But unless she balances within herself whatever is causing her to judge being in the limelight as bad, she will not allow herself to be put in a situation which, on the surface, she feels is "undesirable". She may be missing out on a very important experience that her soul desires her to have—one that would give her enjoyment and satisfaction.

Meanwhile, in an attempt to urge her to become aware of her capacity to be comfortable in the forefront, Elizabeth's soul will continue to replay the drama. It will continue to draw, to her, people who delight being in the limelight. Of course, Elizabeth will wonder why she keeps attracting such annoying people into her life. What did she do to deserve such ridiculous exhibitionism around her? She will attempt to shut out the very people who could help her reclaim this amazing part of herself.

If what we see in another calls forth a strong "negative" emotion or reaction, it is probably something that is out of balance, hidden, denied, or rejected within us.

If what we see in another calls forth a strong "negative" emotion or reaction, it is probably something that is out of balance, hidden, denied, or rejected within us. Those closest to us tend to be the clearest mirrors, because they are able to trigger things well below the surface. For example, an individual who has deep issues of anger may have an angry parent, marry an angry person, or have an angry child. This was, in fact, Greta's situation.

Normally very even tempered, Greta hardly ever became angry. She would "bite her tongue" when something bothered her, not letting the people around her know that what they were doing was upsetting her. There were times, however, that Greta would get so fed up that she would finally explode in an angry outburst. Greta was very good at hiding her anger, but occasionally the steam had to be released.

Greta's husband and son, on the other hand, both became angry very easily. If anyone overstepped their boundaries, they would let him or her know in no uncertain terms. Greta had a difficult time with this. She thought anger was somehow wrong, harmful, or simply "not nice". She didn't think people would like her if she became angry, and she was uncomfortable being around the angry drama of others.

Greta's husband and son were wonderful mirrors for her. It took her a long time to realize this, because she was in projection. Eventually, when she turned the mirror around, Greta saw her own anger. As she came to acceptance of that part of herself, she was also able to see that her anger was a gift that showed her where she needed to set boundaries. Setting clear boundaries was more honoring to her, and less confusing to those around her. Greta learned to use her anger in a positive and balanced way.

As Greta's anger came into balance, the people around her began to balance their anger too. Their job as mirrors in that regard was complete. "Groundhog Day" was over. Life became much more enjoyable, and less dramatic, for everyone.

As we balance our own internal issues, people no longer trigger us in those areas. The "button" is removed. We also attract fewer and fewer people having those issues, because the need for the mirrors they provide for us is gone. The first step toward balancing ourselves is to step out of projection and into the role of observer. You will learn the other steps as you progress through this book.

The first step toward balancing ourselves is to step out of projection and into the role of observer.

Projection is a vicious circle that takes us nowhere. It destroys our relationships, fills our lives with judgment, and hinders our self-awareness. When we turn the one-way mirror around to use it as a mirror to our inner self, we initiate a powerful process of learning, healing, and integration. Each revelation helps to open us up more to others and ourselves—judging less and enjoying more. You can see how it works in the exercise below.

Exercise – Reversing the One-way Mirror

1. *Get into a quiet space and ground yourself.*
2. *Think of someone in your life who annoys or angers you. What is the behavior or trait that you find so annoying? Write it down.*
3. *Ask your soul to reveal to you what this person is mirroring to you about yourself.*
    - *Do you occasionally exhibit the same behavior?*
    - *Is this trait something that you have judged as bad, being very careful not to exhibit it yourself? Has this caused you to go to the other extreme?*
    - *Is there something about this trait or behavior that is unbalanced within you? If you were to balance it, what would you be able to do with it to enhance your life?*

The Plot Thickens

Using others as mirrors for us is a very important tool for self-observation. The one-on-one, focused, interactions we have with others are daily communications from our soul, enhancing our awareness of who we are as we observe what we admire or reject in those around us.

Now let's expand our powers of observation even further, beyond what we can notice through our reactions to other people. Sometimes we find ourselves in situations that seem to be unworkable, uncomfortable, painful, or destructive. They may be situations that happen again and again, and we can't understand why. They may involve several people, or no people at all. These are usually situations where the soul is trying to reveal to us something about ourselves that is in need of healing. It may be a distorted belief system, a harmful behavior, a destructive attitude, or a deeply seated fear. We will use, as our example, the fictitious story of Ted, a very competent and successful engineer.

Ted works for an engineering firm. He has managed many projects for his company in the past, and they have gone quite smoothly – done before deadline and under budget. Currently he is working on one of the largest projects his company has ever contracted. This project was given to Ted to manage because of his successful track record and experience. In the past, Ted has managed the smaller projects by coming up with the design himself and then utilizing the junior engineers to attend to the details of carrying it out, reporting back to him as each step was completed.

This project was different. It was too large for one person to conceptualize all of the little nuances and fine details that needed attention in its design. So Ted and his boss decided to use a team approach, with Ted as team leader. It has not been going well. They are falling behind schedule and don't seem to have a clear direction. The meetings go on for hours, but very little seems to be accomplished. Ted's boss is getting nervous and is putting pressure on Ted to get the job done.

There is a pretty good drama going on here. Although this particular scenario is made up, it is one that is fairly common in the working world. Many of us have been in similar situations where things haven't worked out as planned, resulting in added stress, frustration, chaos, confusion, and delays.

At this point, Ted has a choice to make. He can choose to blame someone or something for the delays, or he can look inward to discern why his soul has brought this situation into his life. Ted can use this as an opportunity to learn something about himself. He can assume the role of observer to come to awareness of what within himself is asking for acceptance, healing, or change—something that would not only enhance his own personal growth, but would contribute to the unity and effectiveness of the group.

Things don't happen by accident. It is possible for everyone on the team to learn from this situation. Ted's job, however, is to find out what his soul is trying to tell him about himself. It is not his job to fix everyone else. Even when we think we can "see" the problem that exists with another, it is more important to determine what, if anything, the situation is teaching us about ourselves. That means taking on a dual role—actor and audience, participant and observer.

Any number of things could surface when Ted looks inward. He might find that he wants things his own way, doesn't trust others' decisions, and lacks flexibility, all of which could destroy the collaborative effort of the team. Or he might feel that he needs to be "the best" to prove himself, or thinks he must demonstrate that he knows more than anyone else (since he is in charge), or needs to have all the answers to be good enough. This team "upset" is a tremendous opportunity for

Ted to understand and mend any number of things within himself.

Different pieces of information are likely to surface at different times in our lives, depending on what we are ready to acknowledge, balance, and integrate. This time, Ted may discover that every person's input is important, no matter how unusual it might seem. In six months a similar situation might teach Ted the importance of releasing control. A year from now, he might see that there is nothing he needs to do to "prove" himself as a worthy person.

It is tempting to want to fix our external problems as quickly as we can. Ted's first impulse might be to resolve the drama surrounding the team. But from the soul's point of view, the real benefit takes place, not when we find a solution to the external problem, but when we use the problem to learn something about ourselves. I have personally found that when I address the inner issues first, the outer issues and circumstances resolve themselves naturally.

The real benefit takes place, not when we find a solution to the external problem, but when we use the problem to learn something about ourselves.

The soul can help us to shift our perspective from the drama that is taking place around us to what is transpiring within. It can use a particular circumstance in a myriad of ways, so it is always good to go within and ask the soul what is to be learned.

On the next page are situations that can occur in people's lives and common reactions to them. In the second column are some suggestions of information or lessons that the soul might be bringing to an individual's awareness through the drama. These scenarios are not meant to give specific answers, but rather to show how one can "rethink" what is being played out.

The Situation and Initial Reaction	The Soul's Perspective
Someone brings to my attention a "flaw" I have in my physical body. My first inclination is to be hurt or angry over his or her rude and inconsiderate behavior.	Is he or she pointing out something that I have not fully accepted in myself? My soul may be asking me to accept my body as it is, unconditionally.
I am out with a group of people. We become separated, and I am left to find my own way home. I am hurt, afraid, and angry with my friends.	Do I have issues of abandonment —of being left with little or no emotional or physical support? Do I feel isolated? Do I trust the Universe to provide for me?
It seems like my parents want to control my every move. My life doesn't feel like my own. I am not allowed to make my own decisions. I want to run away.	Am I willing to be responsible for my own life, or do I need to blame someone else for my difficulties? Do I run away from my problems, rather than looking them squarely in the eye? Am I willing to stand up for myself, or do I rely on others to do it for me?
I lose my home and possessions in a natural disaster. A feeling of hopelessness sets in. I feel like a victim of circumstance.	What new beginnings might my soul be asking me to make: simplify my life, move to a different area, change my lifestyle, focus less on the externals and more on my inner life?
I set a goal for myself, and fall short of achieving it (ex: acing a test, getting a certain job, making the football team, landing a big account, etc.). I feel like a failure.	Was the goal the intention of my soul or my ego? Were there ways that I sabotaged myself in my pursuit of the goal? Am I to redirect my efforts in a different direction? Upon what do I base my self-worth?
My boss continually uses money to threaten or to motivate me. I am angry and afraid that I might lose my job.	What is this telling me about my attachment to money, my security issues, or my commitment to my choice of work?

Now take a situation in your own life with which you are currently having difficulty. It may be a relationship, dilemma at work, family problem, irritating circumstance, health issue, or whatever else is bothering you. The following exercise will help you to use the situation to learn something about yourself.

Exercise – Being the Observer

1. *Begin by grounding yourself.*
2. *Choose a situation in your life that has been difficult for you. It may be a one-time event, or something that occurs regularly. It may involve specific people, or it may be a situation that just keeps happening to you (like getting lost, stranded, cheated, having things break down, getting into accidents, etc.)*
3. *Pretend you are watching a play. Take note of the events as they play out. Imagine that everyone in the scene is an actor, including yourself. You are in the audience, observing the dialog, behaviors, and reactions of those on stage.*
4. *Pay close attention to the actor who represents you in the play. As the play is reenacted in your mind, write down what you do, what you say, how you react, and what triggers you emotionally. Run the play as many times as you wish to get down all of your observations. Be as objective as you can possibly be in your observations.*
5. *Write down everything that triggered a reaction or emotional response from you, such as specific words that were used, names you had been called, actions that were taken, or circumstances or events that happened. Record what others are doing as they relate to you, if it helps to clarify a reaction you have had to them (ex: Harry yelled at me, so I left the room).*
6. *Ask your soul to show you what might be the underlying issues that are "up", for you to heal regarding this situation. Is there a belief that is self-limiting, a behavior that is causing harm to others or yourself, an attitude that undermines your intentions, or a deep-seated fear that prevents you from being your most powerful or loving self?*

When we receive information, we are confronted with another choice—what to do with it. We can believe it or reject it. We can act on it or suppress it. When we obtain the information from our own souls we are more likely to believe it and act on it than when someone else points it out to us. When we act as observers of our own lives, the soul brings things to our attention in the timing that works best for us, too. It would be impossible to deal with all of our issues at the same time. The soul brings them to our awareness in the timing that is appropriate for us to deal with them.

All the World Is a Stage

Let's take our tool of observation one step further, to the world stage. We tend to complain about our political leaders, the things that go on in Congress, the indiscretions of those in authority, the battles between and within countries, and the inhumane treatments of people that go on throughout the world. But what are the people in charge, and the situations they create, telling us about ourselves? What roles are they playing for us?

We'll take a very well known example: that of the travesties that happened in Europe in World War II. It was no accident that Adolph Hitler came into power when he did. He was mirroring for all of us the tendency we have to think we are better, or worth more, than some, and worth less than others. He carried it to an extreme. But until he did, people kept looking the other way. They refused to hold up the mirror he was presenting to them—until it grew well out of hand.

When we as nations chose to do something about the atrocities, we took a step forward in our own personal evolution, and the evolution of the world. Many situations around the globe, having to do with the equal rights of all people, have come to our attention in the last century. With each one, the consciousness of the world has been raised. As a result, we are coming closer and closer to acknowledging and experiencing the equality and unity of all people.

When government leaders pass laws that honor every person, that take responsible care of the earth, or that reduce violence and warfare, they are really mirroring for us the progress we are making as a whole. When they take actions that do the opposite, they are mirroring that for us too. It is up to each one of us to resolve the inconsistencies within ourselves to create a world that loves, honors, and respects all of creation. When we do that, we will choose leaders who do the same. For they are a reflection of ourselves, playing the roles they have agreed to play.

Our leaders are a reflection of ourselves, playing the roles they have agreed to play.

Take a moment to reflect on the current events of the day and your reactions to them. What are the actions of those in power telling you about yourself? What are the prevalent group thought forms and behaviors that are coming to our attention? What can you do to change within the undesirable things that are happening without? What are you being called to balance and integrate?

Being the observer of all that goes on in our lives is critical to our healing and evolution. It is the way that we learn about ourselves through our life's drama, whether the situations are personal or global. It helps us to uncover the issues that prevent us from embracing our emotions and sensuality, that cause our relationships to fall apart, and that keep us from enjoying life.

Self-observation is also the tool we will use to uncover the issues that are lodged in all of the other chakras—issues that prevent the chakras from functioning optimally and that create limitation and pain in our lives. But what do we do with these issues once they are brought to our awareness? How do we actually heal them and mend our lives?

The issues that surface oftentimes have karmic roots. Resolving the karma behind them helps us to move forward through these issues more quickly, bringing relief from the painful situations that keep showing up in our lives. It is also a very good way to reclaim our natural power, as you shall see next.

> The soul simply wants to be itself.
>
> When the third chakra is open and balanced, the soul is free to be what it is.
>
> It wills a life that is in alignment with the divine plan for the soul, and it supports the best and highest good of all.

welcome to

The Third Portal

to your soul...

The Third Portal

Name	Third or Solar Plexus Chakra
Location	Pit of stomach
Traditional Color	Yellow
Functions	• Generates the will and power of the soul • Sets boundaries
Balanced Tendencies	Expression of sovereignty and personal power; honoring of self; self care and nurturance; responsible; assertive; courageous; ability to follow through
Unbalanced Tendencies	Acts out of obligation or guilt; easily intimidated or manipulated; unable to say no or stand confrontation; unable to set appropriate boundaries; unmotivated; insecure; aggressive; egotistical;
Physical Problems	Stomach ulcers; intestinal tumors; diabetes; pancreatitis; indigestion; extreme weight gain or loss; hepatitis; cirrhosis
Mental and Emotional Issues	Controlling or controlled; belligerent or passive; egocentric or little sense of self; personality and eating disorders; victim mentality; codependent
Restoring Validations	I honor myself. I listen to my feelings. I deserve to nurture myself. I am responsible for my life. I am a sovereign and powerful being.

PORTAL #3

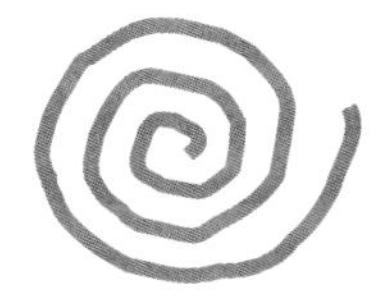

Reclaim Your Life by Resolving Your Karma

Do you sometimes feel as if your life is not your own? Does it seem like there are unseen forces that cause certain painful situations to keep happening to you again and again? Do you find that, no matter how much thought, effort, or planning you put into these endeavors or relationships, they inevitably end up in failure or heartbreak?

If this sounds familiar, it is time to take your life back by resolving your karma. Karma plays a major role in most of the things that cause us to suffer: loss of health, home, job, or wealth; self-sabotaging behaviors; low self-esteem; hurtful and broken relationships; and emotional and mental turmoil.

What is this mysterious thing called karma? How do we get it? What is its purpose? And what do we do with it once we have it? These and many other questions will be answered in this chapter. You will learn how to reclaim your life by paying attention to and resolving the karma that no longer serves you and which creates turmoil in your life.

Not all of our karma is troublesome. Some of it can also be the reason why wonderful things happen to us: why we suddenly win the lottery, are successful in business, or have something nice done for us. The following true story from my own life is an example of this kind of karma.

It was a cold, windy, fall Chicago evening. I was on my way home from work. A loud bang startled me, and my car began to swerve. After the initial shock, it became apparent that the rear tire had blown out. Taking my foot off the gas pedal, I allowed the car to slow down and pulled off the crowded expressway onto the shoulder. I stepped out into the biting wind, opened the trunk, and prepared to put on the spare tire. Within minutes, a man about 10 years older than I pulled up behind me and offered to help. It was obvious that he had honorable intentions. I told him how much I appreciated the assistance. I certainly wasn't looking forward to doing that job by myself. His response to me was, "Well, if my wife were stranded like this, I would hope that someone would stop to help her."

When he said that, my thoughts immediately recalled the previous summer when my two young children, their father, and I were on vacation. We were headed home, driving across a rather desolate stretch of highway in South Dakota. Without warning, my husband pulled over and stopped the car. I asked him what happened. He said there was a woman parked on the shoulder on the other side of the freeway. Since there weren't many cars going by, he thought he'd better see if she needed help. He left the air conditioning on in our car and walked across the divided highway, in the searing heat, to find a woman who had locked herself in her car. She rolled the window down about an inch to talk with him. She had a flat tire, but was afraid to change it. She told him that the last time she did, she had put it on backwards and the guys in the gas station had laughed at her when she pulled in. She wasn't about to go through that again. He changed her tire for her while she waited in her car, and then sent her on her way.

This is an example of karma that feels good. Only months after my husband had helped this stranded woman, a total stranger was helping me in a similar situation. Believe me, it was wonderful to be the beneficiary of that act of kindness. I have been aware of the return of karma like this on many occasions. For years, we took Thanksgiving food baskets to the poor. Then one year we were the recipients of a Christmas basket during a particularly difficult time, when we were living on our savings. Another time, I began to receive large tips from my clients soon after I had begun to tip fast food servers. Over the years, as so many people do, I have helped a number of people move, taken casseroles to the grieving and ill, and offered emotional support to those going through difficult times. Others have generously done the same for me under similar circumstances.

I'm sure you have also experienced karma like this in thousands of wonderful ways. Think about times when others opened the door for you, gave you a smile or an encouraging word, visited you in the hospital, or did you a favor. It felt good, didn't it? You were feeling what others felt when you did the same benevolent things for them. It would be great if all of our karma were like this. We would be delighted!

But there is plenty of other karma that doesn't feel so good. Most of the time we don't recognize it as karma and we can't understand why it is happening to us. Many end up feeling like innocent victims of circumstance. We wonder why "bad" things sometimes happen to "good" people" or why life suddenly takes a detour down a bumpy road. It may be the result of karma.

Can you think of times when you felt like the victim of circumstance or were on the receiving end of the hurtful behavior of others? Maybe it was something simple, like a dirty look, a snide remark, or gossip behind your back. Or maybe it was something more serious, like a string of accidents, physical problems, or financial losses. It could even be something that has haunted you throughout your life in one form or another—like the cruelty of abusive parents, class bullies, violent spouses, or obnoxious bosses. Karma can show up as a series of minor, annoying incidents, or as major tragedies in one's life. Perhaps you are going through something right now that is adversely affecting your life, and you can't understand why. It may be karma.

What Is Karma?

Karma is a sort of "pay-back" system. It ensures that "what you sow, so shall you reap." Karma provides a way for us to experience for ourselves the things we have done to or for others. It teaches us about ourselves by showing us how our actions affect others. These lessons will occur again and again until the lesson is learned.

Karma is a sort of "pay-back" system. It ensures that "what you sow, so shall you reap."

We have been living in a world of opposites (also called polarity or duality). In our creation, there are "two sides to the coin". Karma ensures that we will experience both, if we have experienced one or the other. If we have hurt others in some way, karma ensures that, at some point, we will suffer that same kind of hurt.

If we have been greedy and hoarded our wealth, for example, karma will draw to us one or more situations where we will feel the effects of the greed of others upon us. If we have abused our spouses, children, or employees, karma will turn the table to bring that abuse back to us. If we have ridiculed or judged others, we will undergo the ridicule and judgments of others toward us. Karma draws to us the circumstances and people that can help us experience the other side of the coin and thereby "complete our karma".

We couldn't know the effects of these behaviors upon others unless we have experienced them ourselves. It would be like watching another bang his thumb, and trying to empathize with the pain, when we had never done such a thing, ourselves.

If we have been a blessing to others, karma ensures that we will experience that too. If we have helped someone in need, karma will present us with an opportunity to feel what it is like to be helped when we are in need of it. If we have shown acceptance, kindness, and care toward others, we will be the recipients of these behaviors. Karma helps us to make informed choices about our actions, based upon our experience of how we feel when similar things are done to us. It helps us to live with more love and compassion.

> Karma helps us to make informed choices about our actions...
> It helps us to live with more love and compassion.

Now you might be thinking, "But I never did such and such to other people. I never treated anyone this way. So why is this happening to me? What did I ever do to deserve *this* (whether good or bad). You might either feel like a victim of circumstance or feel undeserving of the kindness of another.

The Payback

Let me explain something about karma. Karma has no time limits. The payback (or karmic return) for our actions can come today, tomorrow, next week, next year, or in the next lifetime. Because of this, we often have absolutely no recall of what caused the karma.

For example, let's say that Tom cheated someone when he was 20. Through karma someone else cheats him when he is 60. Tom may have forgotten all about his fraudulent behavior at 20, or might not see the relationship between the two incidents.

After all, they involved two totally different people. So Tom ends up feeling like a victim at age 60.

The feeling of being a victim becomes even worse when the karmic return appears to be happening lifetimes later, and there is absolutely no recall of any action that would have precipitated the karma. It is not necessary to believe in reincarnation to resolve one's karma. The concept of having multiple lives has gained wider acceptance in recent decades, so it will be included in this discussion. According to one study, at least 60 percent of Americans consider reincarnation a reasonable probability. Another study indicated that 24 percent of Europeans believed in reincarnation in 1990.[1]

Having multiple incarnations would help to explain why some people are "born angry", or have certain issues, behaviors, or memories of events that cannot be related to occurrences from this lifetime. In the work I do with people, past lives are frequently discussed, as situations from other times and cultures come to their remembrance. In my opinion, it is possible that "the other side of the coin" is being acted out in this lifetime. Should that be the case, it is no wonder that so many people feel like victims of circumstance.

When resolving karma, the important thing is not whether we believe in reincarnation. The important thing is to get past the feeling of being a victim. When we feel like a victim, we tend to place blame on another instead of looking within to understand ourselves, as you were shown how to do in Portal #2. We forget that we are simply experiencing the other side of the coin. Coming to an understanding of ourselves and learning the lesson of the karma is a critical component of resolving it. Until we do, the karma keeps repeating itself day after day, year after year, and perhaps even one lifetime into

---

[1] European Value Systems Study: http://www.spiritual-wholeness.org/faqs/reinceur/reineuro.htm

the next, until the lesson is finally learned and the karma is resolved.

Taking Responsibility

When we feel like victims, we do not take responsibility for our karma. We tend to do things that are counterproductive. We might wallow for a long time in our misery. Or we might try to take revenge, creating even more karma. Or we might attempt to run away from our karma thinking that, if we remove ourselves from the situation, the problem will be solved. We may quit our jobs, end our relationships, or move to a different neighborhood, thinking that others are at fault and a change will solve the problems we've encountered. But unless we take responsibility for our karma, learn the lessons that are being offered, and heal within ourselves the issues that are behind the karma, we will eventually fall into the same situations again.

Unless we take responsibility for our karma, learn the lessons that are being offered, and heal within ourselves the issues that are behind the karma, we will eventually fall into the same situations again.

This explains in part why some people go from one sticky relationship to another, get fired from a whole string of jobs, or have certain difficulties for a major portion of their lives. It is also why "bad luck" seems to run in streaks. There sometimes seems to be an endless cycle of repeated negative encounters, painful circumstances, physical problems, or failed endeavors.

When we take responsibility for our karma and stop blaming others for our pain, we can more easily take action to resolve it. When we resolve our karma, we can finally break free of the cycle of pain and mend our lives. This allows us to live a life that is less stressful, healthier, and more fulfilling.

In the last chapter, you learned how to bring to your awareness the internal issues that keep you from living life to its fullest, or that cause you to suffer. In this chapter you will learn how to heal those issues and resolve the karma that may accompany them. This will bring a great deal of relief to the suffering in your life. It will help you to reclaim your life, giving your soul the freedom to create a life of greater ease and joy.

> When we resolve our karma, we can finally break free of the cycle of pain and mend our lives.

Karma and the Third Chakra

Resolving the karma that is located in the third chakra is essential to reclaiming one's life and living a life of joy. For this is the portal through which the will and power of the soul's essence come forth. If this chakra is closed due to karma, the soul's power is diminished; its will is distorted; and the divine plan for the soul's life is compromised. The soul is prevented from living the life it came here to live, and its joy is decreased.

The soul simply wants to be itself—no more and no less than any other energy form. When the third chakra is open and balanced, the soul is free to be what it is. It sets boundaries that are honoring to self and others. It wills a life that is in alignment with the divine plan for the soul, and it supports the best and highest good of all.

Many use the word "sovereign" to describe this state. Personal sovereignty is the state of "being in one's essence", and allowing one's life to align with, and proceed from, that essence. It feels like a very powerful state because the soul's energy is so strong and effective.

> Personal sovereignty is the state of "being in one's essence", and allowing one's life to align with, and proceed from, that essence.

Being sovereign in this sense is personally empowering, and has nothing to do with the control of one person over another.

When the third chakra is closed, the soul's power is usually hidden. This causes the individual to feel weak, powerless, incompetent, or intimidated. He or she may not be able to set appropriate boundaries. There may be little sense of self, and one's life may be driven by the demands of others or by one's own ego, rather than by one's soul.

When the third chakra is unbalanced, the ego may try to take command, using the soul's power to try to control others or life's circumstances. The ego may have a different view from the soul of what is important in life. It may act out of fear, guilt, greed, or a sense of insecurity. This can cause the ego to be selfish in its decrees—to the detriment of others, the planet, the Universe, and even oneself.

The Telltale Signs of Karma

How can we tell whether we have karma to resolve? Karma has many telltale signs of which we can be aware. As was already mentioned, when something unexpectedly wonderful or painful happens to us, it may be the result of karma. If the painful event occurs multiple times, it is most likely due to karma.

> When something unexpectedly wonderful or painful happens to us, it may be the result of karma.

Emotional Signs

Karma usually has an emotional component. This is because, behind the karma, there are usually internal issues to be resolved, as was discussed in the preceding chapter. Emotions that indicate that we have somehow limited ourselves or are acting out of fear are signs that we have issues to be healed and possibly karma to resolve. This is especially true if the same distressful emotions surface repeatedly. Rather than becoming stuck in emotions such as guilt, shame, timidity, depression, distrust, and anxiety—or ignoring them—we can use them to help us uncover the issues and karma that are causing them.

The third chakra is sometimes referred to as the "emotional center". Many of our emotions are felt here, including the powerful emotions of courage, strength, fearlessness, and dignity, and the disempowering emotions of resignation, guilt, and helplessness. Other emotions are felt in other chakras. Trust, betrayal, physical passion and desire are felt in the second chakra; love, compassion, joy, and judgment in the fourth chakra; embarrassment, shame, humility and pride in the fifth chakra, to name a few.

Many of the emotions that we call "negative" are felt in the third chakra. They are not "bad", as we have labeled them. They are important signals to us that we are not fully living from the essence of our souls, have become disempowered in some way, or have denied a part of ourselves. They can be signs that it is time to resolve some karma and reclaim a part of our lives.

For example, we feel hopeless when another's will takes the place of our own. We feel angry when our boundaries are violated. We feel guilty when we don't meet certain expectations. We feel anxious when we doubt our ability to do something. If feelings such as these surface regularly, or persist for long periods of time, it is a sign that we have lost some of our power and that there is karma to be resolved.

It is difficult to support our soul's will for our life when there are issues and karma in the third chakra. The emotional energy of the third chakra is the driver for bringing forth

It is difficult to support our soul's will for our life when there are issues and karma in the third chakra.

our will. This is the energy that carries our intentions and desires into the Universe to be created and manifested. Energy from the third chakra works through the first and second chakras to create and attract to us the people, circumstances, and things that support our will. Issues and karma in the third chakra can weaken this energy. Depending upon the nature of the karma, it can also cause the energy that is there to be used to manifest the desires of the ego rather than the will of the soul.

Issues and karma in any of the first three chakras can distort the energy of manifestation into a darker form that attracts the opposite of what is needed or intended. The karma that is causing the dark emotions must be addressed first. Otherwise it may be difficult to manifest our intentions, to create abundance, or to complete a goal. Consciously we might intend for something to happen, but unconsciously intend the opposite so that the karma can present itself and be resolved.

> Issues and karma in any of the first three chakras can distort the energy of manifestation into a darker form that attracts the opposite of what is needed or intended.

Circumstances that support the karmic lessons causing the dark emotions are drawn to us, even if they sabotage what we have willed. We may create wonderful things, only to have them destroyed by karma. There is a feeling of "taking one step forward and two steps backward". Someone might build a beautiful home, for example, only to have it taken away by fire, foreclosure, or high taxes. Another might land the job of his or her dreams, and then be laid off through downsizing or company closure. Still another might build up a sizable nest egg, and lose it all to poor investments.

One can feel overwhelmed and tossed about by circumstances such as these. But the frustrating and painful circumstances of our lives, and the dark emotions that accompany them, can be important signals that there is karma to be resolved.

Physical Problems

Physical symptoms in the body are yet another of the telltale signs of karma. Recurring physical problems, traumas, and genetic disorders can be caused by karma. Karma will often show up in little ways first. Catching it early can prevent its escalation into a major disease or trauma.

As an example, let's say that Andrea has karma located in her second chakra. The underlying issue for her is the fear of bearing children. Perhaps she overheard a woman describing the pain of childbirth when she was younger, or was exposed to abusive parenting. Or maybe, in another lifetime, she neglected her children, had a stillborn birth, or even lost her own life during childbirth. Andrea may be completely unaware that she has this fear, and may even desire to have children. The fear that is stuck in Andrea's second chakra disrupts the energy flow in Andrea's pelvic area, eventually causing physical problems there.

Oftentimes a particular circumstance or event in one's life will trigger the karma that is already present. For Andrea, the signs of the karma may begin to show up after she reaches puberty. She may have irregular or painful periods. Perhaps she can control the irregularity or pain through medication, feeling that her problems are solved. But then, when Andrea is 28 and trying to have a child, she may have difficulty conceiving. Or she might develop fibroid cysts in her uterus because the karma wasn't addressed when she was younger. Then eventually, when she is older, Andrea may have to have a hysterectomy because her gynecological problems have worsened.

This is an example of how the physical symptoms of karma can grow more severe if the karma goes unresolved. The same kind of escalation of symptoms can occur with mental and emotional problems. The charts at the beginning of each portal contain some of the physical, mental, and emotional signs of underlying issues that may have karmic origins.

DNA Anomalies

Karma can cause anomalies in the DNA, as memories of past events become part of its makeup. Problems that have traditionally been labeled as "genetic" may have a karmic component. For example, if Elliott lost an arm in battle in one lifetime, he might develop a congenital defect in that arm in a subsequent lifetime. If Janine starved in one lifetime, she may have issues stuck in her DNA surrounding the ability to nurture herself. This can manifest physically as liver disease, diabetes, or intestinal problems.

When we resolve our karma, it frees us to heal in many ways, even restoring our DNA if we intend that it do so. Not only can our physical, mental, and emotional health improve, but also the true power and will of the soul can come forth unimpeded. It is much easier for the soul to create a life of ease and joy—one that is in alignment with the divine plan for its life—when we resolve our karma.

Resolving Karma

How do we resolve our karma? We begin by acknowledging it and looking within to learn the lessons from it. This is an important step, so we want to take our time with it. The body provides us with many clues regarding where the karma is located. Aches, pains, and physical problems indicate which of the chakras are affected. Emotional and mental concerns also point toward the location of the affected chakras as well as to the underlying issues behind the karma.

The chakra charts at the front of each portal can help you to begin the process of coming to awareness of the issues involved. But your soul has the real answers. This is not an exercise of the mind. It is one of the spirit. So start by grounding yourself and asking your soul to reveal to you any information that is important for you to understand prior to the resolution of the karma. It may bring up thoughts, feelings, behaviors, or scenes of previous situations. Ask it to help you to understand the issues behind these. It is helpful to write them down.

Keep asking your soul for more information until you feel that the information you have is complete, or until no more information is provided. Then call upon the vibration of forgiveness to do the healing. The healing of the karma happens instantaneously as you call the vibration of forgiveness into your body. It is not a long, drawn-out matter, or one in which you need to get into the "right mind-set".

The physical healing may take longer if there is gridwork to be replaced and tissue to be healed. Usually the gridwork replacement is done while we sleep, since it helps to be still and can be an uncomfortable process. The new gridwork contains information for the DNA regarding the proper construction of the tissue and brings energy to the tissues to revitalize them.

I would like to expound on the vibration of forgiveness. Forgiveness is one of the key energies used to resolve our issues and karma. Forgiveness is the energy of integration. It brings things together. These include people, perceptions, belief systems, emotions, and energies that are typically considered to be at opposite ends of the spectrum. I think of forgiveness as a "zipping" energy. In much the same way that a zipper brings together two parts of a garment, forgiveness

Forgiveness is the energy of integration.

zips up, or brings together, both sides of our karma, resolving it once and for all.

I used to think of forgiveness as a veil of forgetfulness. I envisioned it covering up a failure, indiscretion, or hurt, so that it could no longer be seen. When I forgave someone for what he or she had done, I tried to forget it. But I found that usually the hurt or anger of the situation would return to my remembrance at a later date. I knew I hadn't truly forgiven or forgotten. I would repeatedly try to submerge or stuff the memory and associated pain, but it would eventually come back. That kind of "un"-forgiveness not only doesn't work, but it is unhealthy. The stuffed pain and anger has to go somewhere. It ends up in the body, causing all kinds of physical ailments.

True forgiveness brings together one's experiences, thoughts, and emotions. It integrates them, rather than separates them. For example, one might have a karmic encounter where one person is seen as the perpetrator, and the other person the victim. When the vibration of forgiveness is brought in, there is no separation between the two. Both are simply playing a role to complete a lesson. Forgiveness brings together the two sides of the coin into wholeness. As it does so, the emotional or energetic component of the experience is dissipated. Old resentments, judgments, and other emotional pains are released.

Forgiveness brings together the two sides of the coin into wholeness.

We are living in a particularly exciting time in this creation. Now, more than ever before, we are being given the opportunity to heal our issues, resolve our karma, and live in the power of our souls. The next exercise gives a step-by-step process for resolving karma.

Exercise – Resolving Karma

1. *Begin by grounding yourself. Ask your soul to bring up, from the earth, the vibrations needed to resolve and release your karma—including forgiveness, unconditional love, and compassion.*

2. *Think of a painful situation that keeps happening to you. Maybe you have a chronic physical problem, have been harassed or mistreated in some way, or have had several people take advantage of you.*

3. *Ask your soul to show you what lessons you are to learn from these repeated experiences. Is there some behavior wanting to be changed, some thought forms, beliefs, or emotions ready to be transformed? What about you is coming to the surface to be acknowledged? Is this a reenactment of a situation that occurred a long time ago (where perhaps you played the opposite role)?*

4. *Ask your soul to show you the gift of this experience. What were some of the positive outcomes of it? What did you learn from it?*

5. *Forgive yourself for every situation of a similar nature in which you were ever involved—those in which you felt like the "victim" and those in which you felt like the "perpetrator". It doesn't matter whether or not you remember them. Just set the intention to forgive. Forgive all others involved for the roles they played. Intend to retain the lessons, but release the pain of the memories.*

   Say to yourself, "I release all unconscious agreements, karma, negative thoughts, behaviors, and stuck emotions that no longer serve me surrounding this circumstance and the issues related to it. I intend that they be replaced by thoughts, behaviors, emotions, and beliefs that resonate with who I truly am. I integrate all into balance." It is your job to set the intention. The vibrations coming up from the earth will do the healing.

6. *Feel the vibration of forgiveness running through you. Breathe deeply, releasing the stress, anxiety, and tensions. Feel the lightness of the energy permeating your body and being as you return to wholeness and balance in this area.*

Karma tends to come off in layers. As we rise in vibration through the healing we have done, new layers will surface. These can be new issues, or deeper parts of issues previously released. It may sometimes feel as if one is letting go of the same issue multiple times. In reality, the issue is peeling off in layers from the most surface to the deepest. Trust your soul to do this in the sequence and timing that best serves you.

For example, as I was releasing my own issues related to judgment, the most obvious ways that I judged others and myself were released first. As the months went by, my awareness of judgmental thoughts and behaviors increased significantly. The finer nuances began to surface, as did my awareness of the harm I was creating through the act of judging. As we come to the deepest layers, the actual incident may not be big at all, but it will feel big because the depth of our sensitivity has increased. The lessons that we learn from our karmic encounters become more fine-tuned as we resolve the layers of our issues and karma.

It is important to be patient with ourselves. The karma didn't get there overnight, and we must allow ourselves the time it takes to address it without becoming overwhelmed by it. Healing is a process, not a one-time event. It is through the process of healing that we learn the lessons we are here to learn and mend our lives.

Healing is a process, not a one-time event. It is through the process of healing that we learn the lessons we are here to learn and mend our lives.

Karmic Lessons

Through our karmic encounters, we learn many karmic lessons. We learn how our behaviors affect others as we observe our own reactions to other people's behavior. We learn to what degree we honor ourselves and others, step into our power, and remain sovereign and true to ourselves. We discover our inner qualities, our "strengths" and "weaknesses", our fears, our self-imposed limitations, and the places where we are out of balance.

The charts provided at the front of each portal will help you to understand what types of karma, issues, and karmic lessons are typically located in each of the chakras. The lists are by no means complete, but they will give you a general idea of what each chakra may contain. For your convenience, the karmic lessons related to the three chakras we have covered so far are summarized below.

Karmic Lessons and Issues

First Chakra	Inability to ground Feeling disconnected from the earth or the body Fear of not being able to survive Feeling unsupported Perceived lack of abundance / not having enough Sense of not belonging here / wanting to escape Lack of concern for or appreciation of the body / self-abuse
Second Chakra	Inability to be intimate emotionally or physically Feeling abandoned or emotionally disconnected from others Feelings of betrayal / lack of trust Sexuality issues / sexual abuse Fear of procreation Disdain of men or women Denial of one's masculinity or femininity Inability to mother/nurture others
Third Chakra	Feeling powerless / giving power away Inappropriate boundary setting Controlling or subservient Codependency / competition Ownership of another / being owned Ego directed / narcissistic Lack of self care or nurturing

These lessons may come to our awareness through various problems that arise. Among them are physical, mental, or emotional health issues; self-sabotaging behaviors; debilitating fears; loss of something; accidents; pain and suffering; and disharmony in our relationships.

Each karmic encounter may contain several karmic lessons and issues. Because the chakras work together as a whole, each chakra may hold a different karmic lesson related to the karma that is being played out. Therefore, the physical, mental, emotional, and spiritual effects of the karma may show up in more than one chakra.

Each karmic encounter may contain several karmic lessons and issues.

Let's use, as an example, an individual with a deep-seated fear of not having enough. This may have come about from having gone through a serious economic depression, or a lifetime of starvation (first chakra karmic encounters). The fear of not having enough may show up in that person's life as the inability to keep a job (a first chakra issue); the usury of others to get ahead (a second chakra issue); or a lack of integrity in business endeavors (a third chakra issue). It is sometimes difficult to determine the root cause of the karma because it can show up in so many places. That is why it is important to consult one's soul for the information. I will use the case of one of my clients to illustrate how this is done.

Kurt came to me for a massage to help him relax and to ease the pain in his legs. Kurt couldn't sit still. When I noticed the constant movement, I asked him if he was also experiencing a lot of chatter in his head. He responded with an emphatic "YES!" I asked Kurt what was causing his restlessness. He began by telling me that he was a runner. Running helped him relieve his tension. But his anxiety was mounting because he had stopped running. His left leg hurt too much to run because of some recent mishaps that had occurred while running. He had tripped or run into something on three different occasions and injured his left shin and knee, creating too much pain to run. He was also having problems with his left foot.

The string of accidents was a sign that Kurt was ungrounded. The repeated injuries to his leg indicated that karma was involved, and that it was located in the first chakra. The fact that Kurt's anxiety also increased as a result of the accidents and his inability to run told me that it too was related to the karma. We knew that Kurt was ungrounded and anxious, but we didn't know *why*. We asked Kurt's soul to reveal to us what was causing the injuries and anxiety, and it showed us some very interesting things.

The soul will oftentimes use our emotions to reveal to us the issues that are surfacing as they relate to the lessons to be learned through the karmic encounter. Kurt's soul brought up several emotional responses to the question of why he was ungrounded and anxious.

Kurt suddenly had the feeling of being unable to "stand on his own two feet" financially. It felt like the rug could be pulled out from under him at any time – as if he might suddenly lose everything he had, leaving him destitute. He had the feeling that the Universe would not supply his needs, and that it was all up to him.

These are all first chakra issues. It is no wonder that Kurt was having a difficult time staying grounded. Kurt understood that this was the source of his anxiety. But he couldn't understand why he had these feelings. His current experience should not have caused them. He was successful, talented, intelligent, and on top of things. We asked Kurt's soul to show him why he felt so afraid and unsupported.

Kurt's soul then used Kurt's inner vision, or imagination, to answer this question. It took him back to a scene from what he perceived to be a previous life. He was shown that the rug had indeed been pulled out from under him when he had lost everything he owned in that lifetime.

The fears and emotions of that time had become stuck in his first chakra. If we had looked further, we might also have discovered a lifetime where Kurt had absolutely everything he desired, perhaps at the expense of others or the earth that supported him. When one side of the coin surfaces, one can be assured that the other side of the coin had been experienced too. It is not necessary to "see" that side of it, however, in order to heal the karma. We asked Kurt's soul if there were any more issues of which he should be aware. Another issue was brought to mind.

When one side of the coin surfaces, one can be assured that the other side of the coin had been experienced too.

Kurt was shown that because he had at one time lost everything, he no longer trusted his ability to know what to do. He felt that he needed to rely on someone else for direction. That someone was his wife. She was the visionary – the one who could see in which direction to go. And he was the one who took them there.

Their fears had caused them to become so polarized, that Kurt was no longer in touch with his feminine (visionary) side, and his wife was out of touch with her masculine (manifesting) side. This second chakra issue led to a codependent relationship in which both parties had relinquished some of their sovereignty—a third chakra issue.

Recently, a sort of tug and pull between Kurt and his wife had begun to occur that mimicked the imbalance within each of them. This frequently happens when it is time to integrate one's masculine and feminine sides. The competition may come out as disparaging remarks about men or women, as power struggles, or as statements like: "My ideas are better than yours. I am right and you are wrong. Why can't you think like me? Why don't you get it?"

When we have issues related to our masculine or feminine sides, they will usually manifest physically in the side of the body related to that gender. The left side of the body is the feminine side; the right side is the masculine side. Kurt's feminine issues manifested as pain and injuries to his left leg, knee, and foot. Sometimes one whole side of the body will have physical problems, while the other side remains healthy, as was the case with Kurt.

As was discussed in Portal #1, polarization and competition between one's masculine and feminine sides reverses the flow of one's energy, causing the soul to become ungrounded as it hovers higher in the body. Kurt's inability to ground had at least two causes: 1) the rejection of part of his feminine side, and 2) the fear of not being supported by the Universe.

Kurt's soul had been trying to get Kurt's attention through the series of running accidents. It was pointing to the karma and issues stuck in his first three chakras. Resolving the karmic lessons and issues in his second and third chakras gave Kurt greater sovereignty. These issues involved competition between the sexes and codependency. When he resolved them, Kurt reclaimed his ability to create a vision for his life and bring it into manifestation. This resolved his feelings of insecurity, instability, anxiety, and lack, located in the first chakra. Opening the first chakra in this way helped him to ground, so that he could run again without injuring himself.

Sometimes it is enough to feel the feelings and acknowledge the fears, thoughts, and behaviors that are surfacing to be healed. At other times, the soul may present a picture in the mind, as it did with Kurt, of what precipitated those thoughts and feelings—a reenactment of a previous situation. It does this to make the individual more deeply aware of the feelings and issues related to the karma. It may be from an earlier time in this life, or it may appear to be from a previous life.

The specific pictures that come up, and the timeframes they represent are not, in themselves, the focus of the healing. It is not necessary to believe that the situation actually occurred. It is, rather, the emotions, thoughts, beliefs, and behaviors that surface that are to be addressed. That is why it is not necessary to believe in past lives or reincarnation when resolving one's karma. It can be done, no matter what one's belief systems are.

As we learn our karmic lessons, heal the underlying issues, and resolve our karma, we open our chakras and bring ourselves back to wholeness. It takes diligence to do so, but it is well worth the effort. Life becomes much easier, less stressful, and less fraught with catastrophes and suffering. We repossess our power and our peace and feel better about ourselves. And we give our souls more freedom to create a life that resonates with who we are and what we are here to do.

As we learn our karmic lessons, heal the underlying issues, and resolve our karma, we open our chakras and bring ourselves back to wholeness.

Take It One Day At A Time

Currently, the payback for our behavior (the karmic return) is coming much more quickly than ever before. Perhaps you have noticed this in your own life. I have certainly noticed it in mine. Even the energy of my thoughts, and how they affect those I think about, is coming back to me almost immediately. It makes it much easier to detect and address what is up to be healed.

There is a good reason why the payback is coming so quickly. We are living in a time when the vibration of the earth is increasing very rapidly. In order to keep up with the earth's vibration, we are being given the opportunity to heal ourselves at unprecedented rates. Resolving our karma and issues, and opening our chakras, helps to increase our vibration. If we don't pay attention to and resolve the karma as it comes up, our physical health may decline due to the difference between the earth's vibration and our own. Likewise, as our vibration increases, our health and vitality will improve.

Now, more than ever before, it is critical to take an active role in our healing. Taking it one day at a time and addressing the issues, as they surface to be healed, will keep us from feeling overwhelmed. Otherwise life may begin to feel chaotic and out of control as the number of lessons we are trying to learn begin to pile up and manifest themselves in uncomfortable ways. We should keep in mind that our healing is the most important use of our time. Not only does it result in a healthier, happier life for us, but it also has positive and lasting effects for our world and beyond.

Beyond Karma

Initially there was no need for karma. The human species on earth was fully conscious. It knew, understood, and felt the unity of all. This has been referred to in some traditional religious texts as the "Garden of Eden". In oneness, persons could experience the feelings, joys, and pain of everyone around them as they interacted with each other. All joy was mutual joy. All pain was shared pain. There was no separation of "me" and "thee". Because of this, everyone took care to act in ways that insured the best and highest good of all. People lived in balance, experiencing and learning from one another's emotions and feelings without judgment. The physical experience was one of joy, peace, and harmony—exactly what we are yearning for at this time.

Then humankind fell into density. The balanced energies became polarized into light and dark, creating the experience of good and evil. Humankind began to judge their feelings as good and bad, and found them to be linked to the actions of good and evil. The lack of balance caused a pain that was too great for people to bear as a whole. And so the illusion of separation was created (being cast out of the Garden of Eden). While that perception of separation has kept us from feeling one another's pain so acutely, it has also prevented us from feeling the joy or sorrow that we help to create through our interactions with each other.

Having lost the way we immediately learned about the effects of our behaviors upon others, there was a need to create another way to experience what others experience as they interact with us. That has been the purpose of karma—to teach us the emotional, mental, energetic, and physical consequences of our behavior. Karma has served a great purpose in this creation. It was meant to be a tool for our awareness and healing. But we have suffered enormously from it because we forgot how to use it for these purposes or how to resolve it once we had it.

> We are being called to end the drama of karma. We are at a pivotal point in our history, where we are transiting from the illusion of separation back to unity consciousness.

Humanity has learned the lessons of separation. We have experienced polarity in the extreme. Now we are ready to return to a state of balance and unity. As we increase and expand our conscious awareness of others and ourselves, the need for karma again disappears. We are currently at a place in our evolution where this is actually happening for many people.

We are being called to end the drama of karma. We are at a pivotal point in our history, where we are transiting from the illusion of separation back to unity consciousness.

A very important element in this transition is compassion. Compassion is the acceptance of our differing thoughts, perceptions, beliefs, circumstances, abilities, and behaviors. It works hand in hand with forgiveness to return us to a state of wholeness and unity.

It is very tempting to judge others and ourselves for the things we have done. But we must remember that *everything*, no matter how painful or evil it has seemed, has served to teach us something. Resentment, hatred, and judgment are counterproductive to the healing process. They keep us separate and hold the karma in place.

The things we have done and gone through have all assisted in our learning about ourselves and life in the third dimension. A compassionate person accepts that. Compassion comes from the heart. In the next portal to your soul, you will learn how to open your heart chakra to make a stronger connection with your Higher Self and bring more love, compassion, and peace into your life. You will learn how to stay calm and centered amidst chaos and change. And you will learn how to remain at peace throughout your healing process.

> The more we live from the heart, the more peace we bring into our lives.

welcome to

THE FOURTH PORTAL

to your soul...

The Fourth Portal

Name	Fourth or Heart Chakra
Location	Center of chest at sternum
Traditional Color	Green or pink
Functions	• Connects physical self with spiritual self • Houses the soul's essence
Balanced Tendencies	Conscious acceptance of self, others, and circumstances; lives in the present moment; compassionate; forgiving; unconditionally loving; peaceful; grateful; knows inner self; feels connected to the soul and Higher Self; balanced heart and mind; integrated spiritually and physically
Unbalanced Tendencies	Imbalance between physical and spiritual; judgmental; defensive; ungrateful; lives in the past or future; out of touch with inner self and Higher Self
Physical Problems	Heart conditions; asthma; problems with the blood, ribs, lungs, diaphragm, thoracic spine
Mental and Emotional Issues	Anxious; obsessively worried; unforgiving; bigoted; jealous; hateful; bitter; overcome with regret
Restoring Validations	I am a beautiful being. I am lovable and loving. We are all equal, but not all the same. I am grateful for my life and all its experiences. The present moment is the only moment I have.

PORTAL #4

Be At Peace by Being Centered

When the two World Trade Center Towers came down in New York City, news reporters described a sense of peace in the aftermath of the horror and devastation of September 11, 2001. Amidst all the fear, grief, rage, and constant news updates of that day, many thousands of people found a place of solace within themselves. A place where, united in spirit, they could express love and compassion – a place where forgiveness and peace prevailed. This place is within every one of us.

People commonly describe "a peace that surpasses understanding" coming over them when they are going through a crisis: the loss of a loved one, the news of a terminal illness, the devastation of a natural disaster, or other calamity. I myself have experienced peace like this on more than one occasion.

When my mother died very suddenly, a peace came over me that carried me through the days of her funeral. There was a love connection, the likes of which I had never before experienced.

On another occasion, I was the passenger in the front seat of a car that suddenly spun out of control while merging onto a dark and wet Chicago expressway. After turning round and round in four lanes of traffic, we stalled facing the wrong way. I remember seeing two sets of headlights coming straight at us out of the dark, and completely surrendering myself to the inevitability of a fatal crash. There was no fear, only peace.

The two cars sailed smoothly around us on either side, as if the whole scene had been choreographed. A break followed, in the traffic, which gave my driver time to re-start the car and safely pull over to the shoulder of the expressway.

I will never forget the peace I experienced on those two occasions. I have no doubt that almost everyone could come up with a similar situation where, amidst a tragic or potentially devastating event, he or she found peace that could not be explained. We are sometimes able to find this peace within ourselves when the circumstances around us are beyond our comprehension or control.

Why, then, is it so difficult to find this place of peace when we are going about living our daily lives—when the baby is crying, the deadline is due, the bills are piling up, or the week's agenda is jam packed with responsibilities, appointments and activities? What is it about normal daily life that leaves us feeling anxious, overwhelmed, fearful, confused, depressed, and depleted?

We have discussed the drama of life and how easy it is to become immersed in the drama. You were shown how to go beyond the drama by becoming the observer. But sometimes the responsibilities of life can get us down. It is tempting to want to control every aspect of our lives—to make them "perfect"—and then to become discouraged when we find that we cannot control. It is easy to allow anxiety, guilt, and depression to swallow us up when we fall short of our ideas of perfection. But that is not the way life is meant to be. This chapter will show you a different way—the way of peace. It will show you how to find the place of peace within yourself amidst the drama, chaos, responsibilities, and ordinary circumstances of your life.

The Place of Peace

Where is this place of peace? The place of peace is found in the heart. That is because the heart is the center of our "beingness". It is often referred to as the dwelling place of the soul.

The heart chakra is the fourth portal to the soul. It is through the heart chakra that our souls connect with their higher vibrational aspects, also known as our Higher Selves. Our Higher Selves are extensions of our spirits that exist in the higher dimensions. The soul, which is the part of one's spirit that is having this physical experience, is not separate from its Higher Self. It is one continuous spirit that extends throughout the dimensions.

Our Higher Selves are made up of a greater amount of light energy than are our souls or bodies. That is what causes them to have higher vibrations. We have access to these lighter energies through the heart chakra, as we draw them in from our Higher Selves. These are the vibrations that help us to heal, harmonize, balance, and be at peace. The more we open our hearts, the more we bring in these energies. The energies of the heart are the energies of peace. The more we live from the heart, the more peace we bring into our lives.

Being Centered

Living from the heart is called "being centered". The traditional way of saying this is to place the emphasis on the word "centered": "being *centered*". But another way to say

> Living from the heart is called "being centered".

and interpret this phrase is to emphasize the word "being": "*being*-centered"; that is, centering ourselves in our "being-ness". When we are living in our being-ness, we are more centered or balanced. For it is in our being-ness that we connect with our soul and Higher Self to find more peace, balance, harmony, and healing. Thoughts run clear, emotions stabilize, and grace takes over. Perspectives shift. Perceptions change. Peace rules. How is this accomplished? By practicing the art of be-ing in the energies that open the heart.

> In our being-ness we connect with our soul and Higher Self to find more peace, balance, harmony, and healing.

Let me show you what a difference this makes. We'll conduct a little experiment. Center your awareness in the area of your heart. Tune in to what you are feeling in that area of your body. Does it feel light, heavy, happy, sad, expansive, closed, stressed, peaceful, or what?

Allow the following words and energies to penetrate your being. Feel what they do to your heart area. The words are:

Love
Gratitude
Acceptance
Forgiveness
Compassion

How does your heart feel? Does it feel lighter, happier, softer, bigger, and more peaceful and expanded? That is because these are energies that open the heart chakra. They dissolve the crusty defense mechanisms that surround the heart. When the defense mechanisms decrease, the heart chakra opens and expands. Energies come through it that raise the vibration of our bodies and make us feel lighter. We are able to make a stronger love connection with others and our Higher Selves.

Now consider another set of words. Allow these energies to penetrate your being and then feel what they do to your heart area. The words are:

Hatred
Resistance
Fear
Resentment
Judgment

As these energies enter your field, what do you feel? Do you feel your heart closing and your body becoming heavier? That is because these are energies that contract the heart chakra and lower the vibrations of our bodies. They form the defense mechanisms that separate us from others and our Higher Selves.

Most of us have become quite proficient at protecting our hearts. We have developed all sorts of defense mechanisms that protect us from the hurts of the world. But in doing so, we have closed our hearts and limited our access to the lighter vibrations of our Higher Selves. This has caused us to house an inordinate amount of dark energy. The result has been that we have become unbalanced, emotionally heavy, and lacking in peace.

We desire peace. We want to lighten our emotional load. We desire to have a stronger connection with others and ourselves. All of these wishes can come true if we will open our hearts, connect more fully with our Higher Selves, and bring more of the light energies in to balance the dark. We can only have peace in our outer lives to the extent

We can only have peace in our outer lives to the extent that we have peace within.

that we have peace within. So let us spend some time discussing how to open our hearts by "be-ing" in the energies of the heart.

Being in the Energies of the Heart

Being in the energies of the heart is a practice that takes focused discipline. The more we do it, the more it becomes a habit that just comes naturally.

Be in the Present

The vibrations of the soul and Higher Self are able to come forth most abundantly in the experience of the present moment. The soul can only "be" in the present moment. The past, the future, and all experiences of time, are products of the mind, not the soul.

Living in the past or constantly anticipating the future can become a habit that destroys our peace. A habit is broken by replacing it with a new habit. A habit that brings more peace into our lives is the practice of staying in the present. That habit is formed by paying attention to our thoughts and redirecting them when necessary toward what we are doing, feeling, and experiencing in the moment it is happening.

We can reflect on the past and learn from it. We can plan for the future and in some ways prepare for it. But we must not live *in* the past or live *for* the future. Living outside the present moment is not living at all. It is missing out on the only moment that we have—the present moment. Being in the present moment means being present or attentive to: where we are, whom we are with, and what we are doing and feeling at the time.

> Living outside the present moment is not living at all. It is missing out on the only moment that we have—the present moment.

What takes us out of the present moment? The mind does when it tries to mentally relive the past or anticipate the future. When the mind takes us out of the present, our vibration changes. It can become chaotic and heavy due to worry, anticipation, nostalgia, and regret. Throughout my life, I have had a tendency to daydream, anticipating and solving problems that have not yet occurred, or reliving scenes from the past. I have even brought myself to tears thinking about and fearing the terrible things that *could* happen to people I love. My natural vibration is one of peace. But when I go into this daydreaming mode, my vibration changes. Other, denser vibrations conceal the peace. My brother, who is sensitive to energies, tells me, "You're thinking again!"

The mind oftentimes takes us out of the present in an attempt to create a "perfect" existence—a kind of ideal fantasy where all problems, past, present, and future are solved or resolved according to the purposes of the ego. It might be a life free of regrets, illness, bills, crying babies, or aggravating relationships. It might be a more prestigious job, a perfect report card, an outstanding achievement, fortune, or fame. It might be a "perfect" body or "perfect" mate. To the mind, perfection is rarely "what is". It is what "could be" or "might have been". It is full of "what if's" and "if only's".

> The mind takes us out of the present in an attempt to create a "perfect" existence.

The soul doesn't look at life that way. Perfection is "what is", no matter what it looks like. Perfection could be getting fired from a job, contracting a serious illness, losing one's life savings, a death, or a divorce. The soul sees present difficulties as opportunities for healing, growth, a change in direction, or increased awareness. The soul makes no judgment on whether "what is" is good or bad. Those are judgments of the mind as it compares each situation with its ideas of perfection.

Creating visions and setting intentions are not the problems. These can be the first steps toward much of the change that we bring into our lives, and which can be very empowering. The problem lies in resenting what is, or what has been. Each experience is a tool of the soul that can be used for our awareness and growth, if we embrace it as such. This does not mean we have to like it. But we lose the lesson and richness of the moment when we try to mentally escape from it or, alternatively, obsess about it. On the other hand, when we embrace "what is", we are really living the experience of the moment. Feeling and expressing *appreciation* for "what is" is called gratitude.

When we embrace "what is", we are really living the experience of the moment.

Be Grateful

Gratitude is a vibration of the heart. Being grateful opens the heart and gives us peace. Gratitude helps us to stay present because, when we are grateful, we are focused on what *is*, rather than on what is *not*. Being grateful is a habit. In any situation we can pick out the things for which we are grateful, or we can focus on the things we dislike. It is our choice. Being grateful gives us a sense of well-being and peace.

Think of a time when you were truly grateful for something in your life. Maybe it was the beauty of a sunset, the taste of a good meal, the comfort of home, the birth of a healthy child, or the love of a caring parent, friend, or partner. How did you feel in that state of gratitude? You may have felt nurtured, fulfilled, loved, calm, or happy. These are feelings that come through when we have an open heart. They enhance our peace.

Now think of a time in your life when you developed a strong attachment for something other than what you had. Your desire for it probably consumed your thoughts. Maybe you wished you had more money or a different car, home, job, or partner. Maybe you wanted to be older or younger. Maybe you wanted to be married or to have children. How did you feel in that state of discontent? You may have felt needy, anxious, deficient, deprived, depressed, unloved, or unfulfilled. These are feelings that come through when we have closed our hearts. They destroy our peace.

Gratitude helps us to feel good about our lives and ourselves, keeping us in the present. When we approach all aspects of our lives with a feeling of appreciation, we are "being in" the vibration of gratitude. Being appreciative and grateful is not only a habit; it is a state of being.

Gratitude also brings more of the things for which we are grateful into our lives. That is because we get what we focus on. When we focus our attention on the things that we don't like about our lives, or the things that we don't want to happen, we actually draw more of those things to us. Worry and fear focus our attention on the undesirable, and draw to us the very things that we fret over. That is why worrying about our loved ones or the future is counterproductive. Being afraid of what *could* happen can actually cause it to happen. It also takes us out of the present moment, and destroys our peace.

> Gratitude brings more of the things for which we are grateful into our lives.

What can we do to end the cycle of worry and fear? How can we keep ourselves from fretting over a downturn in the economy, an unstable stock market, job insecurity, or terrorism? What will help us to stop worrying about our teenage drivers when they are out late at night or whether drugs or gangs will take them away from us? What can prevent us from distressing over predictions of earthquakes, wars, or the end of the world? How do we alleviate our fears of the unknown—fears of making changes, of uncertainty, or instability? This is done by being in the vibration of acceptance.

Be Accepting

Acceptance, another energy of the heart, is the antidote to fear and worry. It brings us out of an imaginary future back to the present moment and to our center. In the present moment, we do all we can, so as to ensure a desirable future. But then it is imperative that we let it go, surrendering to what is and what is to be. The result is peace.

The following exercise is a good way to practice letting go. It is helpful for being in the experience of the present moment, releasing all anticipation and control, and surrendering to whatever comes next. You will need another person to help you with it.

Exercise – Practicing Surrender

1. *Lie down on your back and close your eyes.*
2. *Have your partner loosely hold your wrist with one hand, and support your elbow with the other. Let the weight of your arm be supported by your partner's hands.*
3. *Ask your partner to slowly and gently move your arm at the shoulder joint, changing directions, moving it up and down, back and forth, or rotating it different ways.*
4. *Allow your partner to move your arm for you. Relax it as much as possible. Be aware of any sensations of resistance or control on your part. See if you can completely surrender to your partner's movements.*
5. *Repeat with the other arm.*

It is surprising how much people try to anticipate and control the movement of their arms in this exercise. Most have difficulty relaxing their arms enough to allow the other person to move them without resistance. Some even take control and move their arms themselves. We are so used to taking charge, to doing things for ourselves, that we find it difficult to let go, even in something as simple as this. It is a good practice.

When we do let go, we give our souls much more freedom to create the life that is right for us. The mind cannot predict the future; it can only imagine it, based on what it has learned from the past. The soul, on the other hand, can create a future that the mind cannot even imagine. Because the soul has a broader vision of all possibilities, it has much more freedom and flexibility in its ability to create than does the mind and ego.

When we let go, we give our souls much more freedom to create the life that is right for us.

A conflict of interest sometimes develops between the ego and the soul when the mind tries to predict the future based on past or present circumstances. The conflict worsens when the ego, in collaboration with the mind, decides to take control.

Acceptance ends the conflict between the ego and the soul. When the ego surrenders, it is saying to the soul, "I trust you to draw to me the circumstances that result in our best and highest good." The mind may not understand, in the moment, *why* or *how* a particular circumstance can be for the highest good. Nevertheless, the mind and ego follow the leading of the soul and supports it all the way. Acceptance of this magnitude alleviates a great deal of stress and needless disappointment.

I have experienced many wonderful surprises that my soul had in store for me when I surrendered to its leading. A promotion I didn't get led to the creation of a new position in which I thrived and grew—a position which was far less stressful than the position I thought I wanted. Rejections by publishers and agents for this very book resulted in new lessons learned, revelations, and important changes regarding its format and content. When an organization for which I was a teacher decided not to keep me on, my soul used this as an opportunity to show me my own truth, rather than following someone else's.

> Following the soul's leading, rather than the mind's or ego's agenda, is key to staying on track with the divine plan for our lives. The space that one enters through this kind of acceptance is the place of peace and joy.

Our souls know what they are doing. Following the soul's leading, rather than the mind's or ego's agenda, is key to staying on track with the divine plan for our lives. In every one of these instances, the outcome led me into a deeper experience of myself and my soul's purpose. It was not what my mind had anticipated or hoped for. But it was right for me.

Surrendering to whatever the soul brings forth in the moment opens the door to incredible growth. When we surrender the will of the ego to the will of the soul and Higher Self, we are "being in" the vibration of acceptance. The space that one enters through this kind of acceptance is the place of peace and joy. Perhaps there is presently a situation in your life that your ego is resisting or trying hard to control. If so, you can use the exercise on the following page to help you turn it over to your Higher Self.

Exercise – Being in the Vibration of Acceptance

1. *Think of something about which you are worried, anxious, or stressed.*
2. *Ground yourself and ask your soul and Higher Self to create an outcome that would result in the best and highest good for you and all involved. Intend that this be the outcome, even though you don't know what it is.*
3. *Ask your Higher Self whether there is anything you should do about it now. Is there some step you should take? It may be something small, or there may be nothing at all for you to do. See what comes to mind.*
4. *Run the vibration of acceptance up from the earth through your body and aura, and tell your soul and Higher Self that you surrender to the outcome, no matter what it is.*
5. *If there is something that your Higher Self told you to do, make sure you do it. It may or may not lead to the outcome that your mind envisions, but it will be the next step toward whatever outcome your soul desires for you.*

You will find that the more you practice being in the vibration of acceptance, the more accepting you will be. You will begin to develop a deep trust in and appreciation for the wisdom and leadership of your soul and Higher Self as the stress caused by worry is replaced by the peace of knowing that "everything will be alright".

Acceptance keeps us in the present moment by dissolving the worry and fear of an unknown and "uncertain" future. We can also be taken out of the present moment by stresses from the past. What keeps us from reliving the past? The mind loves to dredge up the past and then beat us up for the "mistakes" we have made. It also takes us back to the hurts that others have inflicted upon us. It reminds us of old wounds, makes us angry all over again, and sometimes seeks revenge.

When the mind focuses on the pains of the past, it fills us with regret, guilt, shame, and anger, and destroys our peace. It usually plays the same tape over and over again with no resolution...because there is nothing to be solved. This can be extremely stressful and wearing.

How does one stop the tape? How is the past healed and allowed to be as it was, so that the mind can stay focused on the present? It is done through forgiveness—another energy of the heart.

Be Forgiving

The vibration of forgiveness was addressed in the last chapter, where it was used to heal internal issues and karma. A forgiving person understands that every life event has served in some way to enhance one's growth, learning, and evolution. This kind of understanding allows the past to be as it was, dissolves guilt and resentment, and opens the heart. In my experience, forgiveness is the major energy used to heal the past.

Let's clear up a few misconceptions about forgiving the past. Forgiveness is not accomplished by painting over the past—erasing it, forgetting it, or hiding it away somewhere. That is not forgiveness; it is denial. Nor is forgiveness the same thing as exoneration, for exoneration implies fault. Forgiveness is not accomplished by analyzing who was right or wrong. That kind of analysis adds the element of judgment to the hurts, regrets, and guilt that are already present.

> When the past is integrated through forgiveness, there is no longer a problem to be solved, an enemy to be tamed, or a wrong to be righted.

True forgiveness is integration. The vibration

of forgiveness takes what was once perceived to be separate and brings it back into unity. When the past is integrated through forgiveness, there is no longer a problem to be solved, an enemy to be tamed, or a wrong to be righted. *There is experience, learning, awareness, growth, responsibility, and choice.*

At the soul level, we understand that the perpetrator and victim work hand in hand, under mutual consent (usually unconsciously). They are like two actors in a play, each carrying out his or her respective role until the message they are conveying finally enters the individuals' conscious awareness to be looked at and integrated. Remember, when a situation occurs, both parties are equal participants at the soul level. Both are learning something or resolving karma by the interchange.

At the soul level, we understand that the perpetrator and victim work hand in hand, under mutual consent.

How is forgiveness accomplished? As you will recall, forgiveness comes forth through one's intent. One forgives by intending to ground and running the vibration of forgiveness up from the earth through the body, the aura that surrounds the physical body, and the circumstances, the people, and the energies involved. It heals the past. It is lasting. And it only takes a moment.

There are times when I feel out of sorts (not centered), and I don't *know* what is causing it. I ground myself and run the vibration of forgiveness through my body and aura, and immediately feel better. It is a quick and effective way to stay centered. The next exercise shows how it is done.

Exercise – Integrating the Past Through Forgiveness

1. *Think of something that bothers you from your past. It can be a recent experience, or one from years back. It might be something about which you feel angry, guilty, regretful, or incomplete. It may involve something you did to another or yourself, or something that someone else did to you.*
2. *Ground yourself and ask your Higher Self to reveal to you what you are to learn from that experience. Did it teach you something about yourself, help you to make different choices, or give you more compassion for others?*
3. *Is there karma to release? Then release it.*
4. *Intend to run the vibration of forgiveness through your body and aura to integrate and heal whatever has been bothering you.*

You can do this anytime something is triggered about the past. Forgiveness heals the past to bring us back to the present moment. It also works on situations that have just occurred. Forgiving immediately, as we observe whatever the soul is trying to teach us through these situations, helps us to stay centered and in the present moment. We are "being in" the vibration of forgiveness when we approach our life's trials, confrontations, and hurts with an attitude of, "What am I being shown here?" and "What roles are being played in order to accomplish this awareness?" Forgiveness helps to keep the heart open, as does its companion vibration: compassion.

Be Compassionate

Like forgiveness, this compassionate energy of the heart has been misunderstood. To many people, compassion has an element of separation to it. It is "normal" to feel compassion for the poor, sick, homeless, and oppressed. But what about having compassion for the wealthy, healthy, powerful, and oppressive? This may seem like an odd question to ask. Why would the latter group of people need compassion? Why would we even want to show compassion to someone who oppresses another?

The confusion lies in our perception of compassion. Compassion has classically been thought of as a "do-ing" energy. We have typically considered the following activities to be acts of compassion: giving food to the poor, shelter to the homeless, medical care to the sick, and comfort to the grieving. But these are actually signs of our caring rather than our compassion. Compassion is a "be-ing" energy. It is an attitude and state of being from which our demonstrations of caring proceed. One can be compassionate without "doing" anything. In fact, compassionate people often do nothing. They don't judge, discriminate, get revenge, or try to change people.

A compassionate person understands that *everyone*, without exception, is here for a purpose. That purpose may include behaviors and experiences that we neither understand nor condone. A compassionate person sees no difference in the value of the life of the oppressor and the oppressed, the rich and the poor, the healthy and the sick, or the criminal and the victim. Compassion accepts that the lessons and purposes of each life are unique, and

A compassionate person understands that *everyone*, without exception, is here for a purpose. That purpose may include behaviors and experiences that we neither understand nor condone.

makes no judgment about those lessons and purposes, no matter how they appear.

That is not to say that we can't have discernment. Our own growth requires that we exercise discernment. Discernment is a balanced combination of assessment and compassion—assessment of the behavior of, and compassion for, the person. The behaviors of others are opportunities for us to assess whether or not we wish to emulate them. In the course of that assessment, we as a society may also see fit to restrain certain individuals from hurting others.

Discernment is a balanced combination of assessment and compassion—assessment of the behavior of, and compassion for, the person.

It is crucial, however, that we maintain compassion toward the individual, no matter what his or her behavior. For when we judge, condemn, or hate an individual for what he or she has done, we close our hearts to him or her. Each time we close our hearts for any reason, we close down the heart chakra a little more, separating ourselves from others, limiting our access to our Higher Selves, and undermining our peace.

We have been living in duality to show us in detail the effects of unbalanced energy. Duality requires that one play the "good guy" and one play the "bad guy". We do not hate the actors that play the roles of "bad guys" in movies. If we are to maintain an open heart and be at peace, it behooves us not to hate our fellow human beings who have played those roles for us in life. We may restrain them, honoring the fact that they have played the dark roles, but we do so in love. That is compassionate living.

When we have compassion, we accept and embrace one another's different roles, abilities, and journeys. We open our hearts to others, no matter what their race, creed, social status, lifestyle, history, or behavior. Compassion values the equality of all people and allows them the experiences for which they are here.

Compassion understands that we are all equal, but we are not all the same. It does not try to make everyone the same. Rather, it accepts the equality of people's differences. When our very thoughts and attitudes reflect this, we are "being in" the vibration of compassion. As was mentioned in the last chapter, compassion is a key element in the healing of our karma and bringing peace to our lives. It is particularly important to have compassion for ourselves. This means accepting that our past behaviors have contributed to our understanding, awareness, and growth. It also means accepting ourselves for who we are.

Compassion understands that we are all equal, but we are not all the same.

Be Yourself

There has been a tendency in our governments, schools, societies, and religions to "homogenize" the people and culture of the organization. Perhaps this was an attempt to find a "pseudo-peace". Or perhaps this was a way to control people. One would think that when everyone thinks and acts the same, there would be less of a tendency toward friction and dissent. But the opposite is actually true.

Deep down in our souls, we know that homogenization is against our nature. We are here to express our uniqueness and to learn how to combine our unique gifts toward the highest good of all. It is very difficult to do that when we are all trying to be the same. So we get angry—very, very, angry. We get angry with ourselves for not being like other people. We get angry with others for insisting that we be like them. We get angry with our parents, employers, and mates for trying to make us into something that we're not. Some take their rage out on the road. Others bring it into their homes, schools, and workplace. Still others commit heinous crimes or become rebels and outcasts. We create a volatile environment by trying to squeeze everyone into the same mold.

More often than not, we submit to the pressure and bury our uniqueness. We develop defense mechanisms against our very selves—walls around our hearts that hide the essence of who we are. We submerge the anger or turn it inward and go about living our lives as we are expected and told to do. We lose our passion for life, as it becomes a mechanical existence. We become depressed (anger turned inward) and sick. Our hearts shut down, and we lose our peace.

We try to make up for the lack of passion in our lives by keeping ourselves busy. We are told that the best way to overcome depression is to stay busy. The advice we are given is: "Don't think too much", "Don't feel too much", "Just stay busy", "Do something 'worthwhile' and you will feel better about yourself". Altruistic activities do open the heart, and it seems to work for a while. But it is never enough. Some people take on more and more until they are totally exhausted or burnt out.

There is a tendency to get so wrapped up in what we are doing that we actually begin to believe that what we do is who we are. When asked who we are, we respond with what we do. We spew off a list of our roles and activities. Then when things change, we wonder who we *really* are. We go through one identity crisis after another as the roles change in our lives—when we go off to school, get married, have children, turn the next decade, become empty-nesters, get divorced, retire, or change careers. We search and search to find ourselves, and frequently come up empty.

Why? Because we are focusing more on our "doing-ness" than our "being-ness". I perform the roles of mother, daughter, partner, writer, massage therapist, and intuitive healer. But that is not who I *am*; it is what I *do*. Plenty of other people do those things too, but they are quite different from me.

We are powerful beings with unique sets of vibrations. A better way for me to portray myself would be to describe the vibrations that make up my being. I could say that I am kindness, calmness, service, tenderness, love, compassion, wisdom, and unity. When I center myself in those vibrations, I am "*being* centered". I express who I am through these vibrations, no matter what I am doing or what life changes I am undergoing. This is the place of peace, joy, true passion, harmony, and healing for me.

The things that I do are integral to who I am. My doing proceeds from my being. We will go into this to some extent in the next chapter, and in great detail in the second book of this series. You will see why, in Portal #6, the "dark" aspects of our vibrations are part of us too, and you will learn how to integrate them into the "whole", balanced you.

Being ourselves – who we truly are – is paramount to being at peace. For peace can only be felt when the heart is open. And the heart can only be open when the vibrations that it houses are allowed to shine forth. These vibrations are the building blocks of our souls, the very fabric of our being-ness. Be yourself, and you will find more inner peace.

> Being ourselves—who we truly are—is paramount to being at peace.

Be Loving

The heart is a symbol of love. Love comes from the heart. Thinking and doing loving thoughts and behaviors open the heart and give us peace. Thinking and doing unloving thoughts and behaviors close the heart chakra and destroy our peace. The energies of the heart, such as the ones described in this chapter, may be called "love light" energies. They are both loving and light. When we are being grateful, accepting, forgiving, and compassionate, others describe us as loving.

> Acts of kindness, caring, giving, and nurturing are some of the "doing" aspects of love.

Acts of kindness, caring, giving, and nurturing are some of the "doing" aspects of love. They help to open our hearts if they are done out of loving energy. They tend to close our hearts, and build resentment, if they are done out of guilt, obligation, coercion, or pride.

Bringing in Love Light Energies

Up to this point, throughout the exercises in this book, you have consciously brought energies into your field from the earth, using your grounding cord. This was done because the first chakra, the one through which we ground to the earth, was the first portal to be addressed and opened. By opening the first chakra and grounding, it became easier to bring in the healing energies.

Love light energies also come in through the heart chakra from our Higher Selves. Whether we are conscious of it or not, there is a continuous energy exchange between our Higher Selves and the earth through all of our chakras, our bodies, and our Auric field. The heart is the "central dispatch" or "hub" for this exchange.

A simple way to visualize this energy exchange is to think of it as a figure eight or infinity pattern. The "top end" of the figure eight goes through the heart of the Higher Self. The central point of the figure eight goes through the heart chakra of the body and soul. The "bottom end" of the figure eight goes through the heart of the earth. There is a continuous flow of energy back and forth between our hearts and our Higher Selves, and between our hearts and the earth. It could be said that we are "grounded" both to the earth and to our Higher

Selves. Of course, in reality the energy exchange is infinite and multidimensional, but it is easier for our minds to grasp the general concept using a two-dimensional, finite model, as depicted in the following diagram.

Bringing the energies in through the heart has the added advantage of bringing in more of the energy combinations that are unique to one's being. It helps to align the vibration of our bodies and aura with that of our souls and Higher Selves. At the same time, it gifts the earth with the vibrations of our Higher Selves, helping to raise the earth's vibration as well as our own.

You have learned how to make a conscious grounding connection between yourself and the earth. How is this conscious connection made between our hearts and Higher Selves? It is simply a matter of intent. We can, for example, imagine a shaft of light connecting the heart with the Higher

Self. An effective way to make this conscious intentional connection stronger, and bring in more of the love light energies of the Higher Self, is through meditation.

Meditation

Many people use meditation to center themselves in their being-ness. In the process, they find peace and raise their vibration. Meditation is a good way to practice quieting our thoughts, worries, and regrets, enabling us to just "be". There are numerous fine books, tapes, and courses available that teach one how to meditate.

Many people use meditation to center themselves in their being-ness.

Some people say, "I have a difficult time meditating. I keep thinking about other things". Others admit that they just don't take the time to do it. These seem to be the two biggest impediments to meditation. The exercise on the following page addresses both of these obstacles. It helps to calm the mind by giving it something upon which to focus so as to quiet its thoughts. And it takes less than 15 minutes to do. It will show you how to work with your breath, which is at the center of many meditation techniques. As an added bonus, it will teach you how to move your body's internal energy, or chi—a benefit to be discussed in the next chapter. This exercise will help you to bring in more of the love light energies from your Higher Self. It is a meditation in its own right.

My brother, Robert J. Lins, who is an M.D, developed this exercise. He has studied alternative and complementary healing modalities for over 20 years. He has used this breathing technique very successfully to calm people who are in high anxiety states, where the mind, emotions, and sympathetic nervous system race out of control. Try it and see how much more peaceful and centered you feel afterwards.

Exercise – Breathing in Love Light Energies

Part I – Heart to Hands Breathing

1. *Obtain a digital oral thermometer—one that is capable of registering a fairly low body temperature—say 90°F.*
2. *Assume a comfortable meditation position and ground yourself.*
3. *Turn the thermometer on and hold the sensing end of it between the thumb and forefinger of one of your hands, resting your hands and thermometer comfortably in a relaxed position. (I hold the sensing end in one hand, and the large end of the thermometer in the other hand, and rest both hands on my lap). You may find that changing hands periodically during the exercise helps, since the hand holding the sensing end of the thermometer may become tense and may not warm up as quickly as the hand that is more relaxed.*
4. *Begin to breathe slowly (approximately 6 breaths/minute). Pause at the end of each out-breath to allow yourself to experience the void. The void is the space where acceptance of all that is around you can most easily be achieved. It is a place of peace.*
5. *With each in-breath, visualize a stream of warm loving light, such as a shaft of sunlight, from your Higher Self, shining into your heart and chest space. As you breathe in, visualize the love light coming into your chest and then flowing up into your shoulders.*
6. *As you exhale, visualize the love light energy flowing down your arms, into your fingertips, and expanding out.*
7. *Notice the reading on the thermometer when you first begin this exercise. If your hands are cold, the surface temperature may not even register, for it may be less than 90°F. But as you continue to breathe and visualize the love flowing through your fingertips, the temperature should rise. Keep practicing daily until you are able to register a temperature of 94°F on the thermometer within five minutes. When you are able to do that, you will know that your breath is moving the chi all the way out to your hands.*

Exercise – Breathing in Love Light Energies

Part II – Heart to Feet Breathing

You won't be able to use the thermometer to give you feedback on this part. After you have been able to do the heart to hands exercise, however, you will have the kinesthetic sense of what it takes to do it. As you breathe in, visualize the love light energy flowing into your heart and chest area, down your spine and into your hips. Then as you exhale, visualize the love energy flowing down your legs and into your toes and expanding out. Practice this until it feels similar to what you experienced in the heart to hands exercise.

This exercise does several things all at once. It calms the mind, bringing it back to the breath, which is what is truly happening in the moment. It connects the body with the soul through the breath. It connects the soul with the Higher Self through the shaft of love light energy. And it moves the internal energy, or chi, in the body. After you have done the exercise, check in with your inner self to see how much more balanced, connected, energized, and peaceful you feel.

The Role of the Heart Chakra

The heart chakra is our connection to our Higher Spiritual Self. Because of this, it has the further function of connecting and harmonizing our spiritual self with our physical self. It does this by acting as the central balancing point for the other six chakras. Chakras one through three deal primarily with the physical part of our existence. Chakras five through seven bring in more of the spiritual side of us. The

> The heart chakra unites and integrates the spiritual with the physical.

heart chakra, which is exactly in the middle, unites and integrates the spiritual with the physical.

The heart chakra helps the first chakra to work harmoniously with the seventh chakra. Through the heart chakra, we combine our ability to create a sustainable physical life (a first chakra function) with the spiritual guidance from our Higher Selves (a seventh chakra function). This results in a life that flows with ease and abundance.

Likewise, the heart chakra helps the second chakra to work in conjunction with the sixth chakra. When our physical sensual input (a second chakra function) goes through the heart chakra to the sixth chakra, it allows us to create a perspective that is in alignment with the soul's truth (a sixth chakra function).

The heart chakra also helps the third chakra to align with the fifth chakra. When the will and power of the third chakra are aligned with the soul's essence in the heart chakra, the individual is better able to create a life that supports his or her soul's purpose, through the fifth chakra.

When the heart chakra is closed, the interaction between the physical and spiritual sides of us becomes impaired. If that happens, one's life will typically function from either the lower three chakras or the higher three chakras. A person who functions from the lower three chakras may be very grounded, successful, and powerful—qualities of the lower chakras. But the lack of input from his or her spiritual side may cause him or her to be ruthless, self-centered, dishonest, and generally out of touch with the higher values of life. The person may also be very unhappy if his or her life is misaligned with the soul's essence and purpose.

On the other hand, a person who functions from the upper three chakras may be highly focused on the spiritual side of life, and quite gifted with spiritual abilities. But the individual may not be able to support himself or herself very well on the physical plane. It takes a balance of both the physical and spiritual to have a successful and fulfilling life that supports both the body and the soul. This balance occurs through the heart chakra.

The heart chakra can only do this job to the extent that each of the other chakras is also open and balanced. For example, if the third chakra is closed, it will be difficult for an individual to fully manifest his or her soul's life purpose, even if the fifth chakra is open. That is because either the drive or will to do so is lessened by the closed third chakra or the will of the soul is undermined by the will of the ego.

The proper functioning of each chakra is dependent upon how well the energy is able to flow in and out of the chakra between the body and the soul. Closed chakras not only impair the joining together of the body with the soul but they also affect the health of the body, mind, and emotions. Each chakra energetically feeds a particular area of the body. The flow of energy to that part of the body is directly related to the openness of the chakra. If a chakra is closed, the flow of energy to that area of the body is dramatically reduced. The result may be physical, mental, and emotional problems related to that area of the body.

There are many reasons why the chakras close and why the flow of energy slows down. Generally, it is said that the energy is "stuck" there. The next chapter will explain what causes our energy to become stuck, and how we can get it moving again. Moving stuck energy opens and enhances the functioning of the chakras and brings in more of the life-sustaining energy needed for the vitality of our bodies. This improves our health and well-being, reverses the aging process, and supports the evolution of our souls. It is a very important aspect of mending every aspect of our lives, including living them in greater alignment with our soul's purpose—a function of the next portal to your soul.

welcome to

The Fifth Portal

to your soul…

The Fifth Portal

Name	Fifth or Throat Chakra
Location	Centered in throat. Encompasses neck, mouth, jaw, shoulders, arms, hands
Traditional Color	Sky blue
Functions	• Speak and live the soul's truth • Carry out the divine plan for the soul's life
Balanced Tendencies	Honest and truthful self-expression; passionate living; sense of purpose; follows one's dreams; uses one's gifts and abilities; openness; integrity; confidence
Unbalanced Tendencies	False display of self; lack of integrity; given to attachments; lack of purpose; loss of meaning; fear of rejection or of being different; chameleonic
Physical Problems	Problems with the neck, shoulders, voice, larynx, esophagus, trachea, gums, teeth, thyroid; sore throat; mouth ulcers; TMJ; carpal tunnel syndrome; tennis elbow; swollen glands
Mental and Emotional Issues	Lying; repression; boredom; denial; abruptness; self-deprecation; self-absorption; overly critical; deluded; frustrated; hopeless
Restoring Validations	My individuality is a gift to all. I have unique gifts and abilities. I have the right to express my truth. I intend to carry out the divine plan for my life.

PORTAL #5

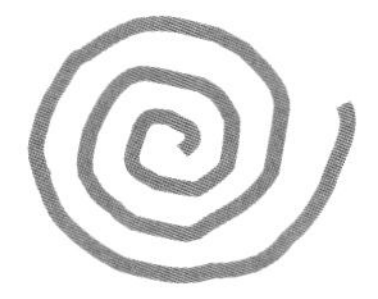

Get Out of the Rut by Moving Stuck Energy

Would you say that your life flows with joy? Do you look forward to the beginning of each new day? Do you enjoy the work and activities that you do? Does your life represent who you really are? Do the people around you support who you are? Are you happy, robust, and healthy?

Or would you say that you're stuck in a rut? Do you wake up each day with a feeling of dread, finding it hard to get out of bed? Are you stuck in a job or situation that doesn't suit you? Do the people in your life tend to put you down? Do you have chronic physical problems that you just can't resolve? Do you feel like you're living somebody else's idea of what life should be? Do you wish you could make some changes? If you're like many people, there may be something about your life that feels like a muddy rut. It could be your job, your health, your home life, your addictions, your relationships, or something else that is causing you to feel stagnant, stuck, and unhappy.

Then there are those days when we just feel "off". Have you ever wondered why some days your body suddenly feels better or worse than it does on other days? Perhaps you have had days when, for "no good reason", you were really tired or "out of it"—and other days when you felt really good. How often do you blame your physical and emotional ups and downs on the weather, hormones, or the things that are going on in your life? Most of us have done that. But there is much more to it than first meets the eye, for these ups and downs are all related to the movement of our energy. Changes in the weather, phases of the moon, hormonal activity, life's circumstances, interpersonal interactions, and other life happenings will affect us most when our energy is stuck at some level. They tend to exacerbate a problem that is already there.

When we start to pay attention to the things that cause our energy to become stuck, and learn how to move the energy again, we begin to have a major impact on the efficacy of our lives. We become less affected by outside stressors. We move forward in the areas in which we have previously been stuck. Our energy, health, and vitality increase. We have the insight and courage to make needed changes. Life becomes much more dynamic, centered, satisfying, and fun as we move out of the ruts caused by stuck energy.

In this portal, you will learn to identify the causes of stuck energy and the ruts it creates in your life. You will then learn how to get out of those ruts by moving your energy. This will help you to create a life that flows with joy.

What Is Stuck Energy?

> Stuck energy is energy that is moving more slowly than it should.

Everything that exists is energy. Energy, by its very nature, moves. Each kind of energy moves according to the frequency of its own vibration. Even the energy in rocks is moving. Stuck energy is energy that is moving more slowly than it should.

When energy slows down too much, it changes the dynamics of the form it comprises. It slows down the vibration of the atoms, molecules, and cells. In plants, it causes decay. In the body, it causes disease and aging. In the mind, it causes confusion and an inability to focus. In the emotions, it causes depression.

The physical body houses its own internal energy system, called chi (chee). Chi moves through the body in a fairly predictable pattern. The pattern is made up of energy channels or meridians. These are not so much carriers of energy as they are a depiction of how the energy itself flows.

Blockages can occur in the pattern of energy channels, causing the chi to slow down, back up, and pool in certain places. That leaves some areas having too much stored energy (such as trigger points) and other areas not having enough energy. This can cause weakness, temperature variations, disease, decay, pain, and a lack of vitality.

In the etheric body (the part of the aura that is closest to the physical body), energy moves through a system of lay lines called gridwork. The gridwork contains a blueprint for the physical body. It works in conjunction with the DNA. If the gridwork becomes damaged, the energy gets stuck there, and the effects of that will eventually be seen and felt as similar damage to the physical body.

Problems that surface in the physical body occur first in the etheric body. For example, if the gridwork of the etheric body is blocked or damaged at the shoulder or behind the scapula, a person may develop rotator cuff problems.

Problems that surface in the physical body occur first in the etheric body.

The Effects of Stuck Energy

Your body lets you know when its energy is moving well or poorly. At a very basic level, we all know what that feels like. We've all had times when we've felt fit and energetic and other times when we've felt achy and lethargic.

As an example, recall a time when your body experienced the wonderful benefits of movement every day. Maybe you walked or rode your bike to work or school. Or maybe you were on a daily exercise routine. Or maybe you had a job or outside activity that utilized the strength or flexibility of your body. Do you remember how good and alive it felt to move every day? Do you remember how in tune you felt with your body, and how much better you felt mentally, emotionally, and physically? That is because you were moving your energy.

Now recall an occasion when you had to be still for a long time. Perhaps you were attending a lengthy conference or meeting and sat for hours on end. Or maybe you took a cross-country vacation, driving in the car for days. Or maybe you were extensively bedridden with the flu or some other serious illness or injury. Do you remember what that was like—how sore, cramped, weak, and stiff your body felt after not moving much for a long time? You were feeling some of the physical effects of stuck energy.

We know what it feels like to experience the effects of stuck energy in these obvious physical ways. But there are many other, less obvious, ways that stuck energy affects us. These can be much more detrimental to our mental, emotional, spiritual, and physical health than the simple lack of exercise, as you shall soon see.

The Benefits of Moving Our Energy

As I have progressively moved my stuck energy, I have seen a positive change in my body, mind, emotions, and life. People tell me I look younger. My skin has taken on a new glow; it is tighter and suppler. I have more energy and stamina. My immune system is stronger. My hips, which used to hurt for days after carrying heavy loads, don't bother me anymore. The daily headaches are gone. My mind is clear. I am almost always in a pleasant mood and I have a renewed enthusiasm for life. Not bad for having passed the half-century mark. And it keeps getting better and better! These are all things that we desire. But there are other very important reasons for moving our stuck energy. These include supporting our evolution, enhancing our energy, and helping us to get out of life's ruts.

Evolution

Moving stuck energy allows the body's vibration to keep pace with the evolution of the soul. As the vibration (or energy level) of the body increases, it allows the soul to be more present in the body. The more present the soul is in the body, the faster the soul can evolve through this physical, earthly experience. The soul must be grounded in the body if it is to benefit from its earthly life.

Moving stuck energy allows the body's vibration to keep pace with the evolution of the soul

Have you ever had an intense spiritual encounter, and the next day felt wiped out, depressed, or came down with a cold? That is because the body wasn't able to handle or maintain the higher vibration that the soul brought into it. Then, when the body's vibration dropped again, the effect of it was felt as a discomfort, illness, or emotional let down. Raising the body's vibration by moving stuck energy allows the body to more easily accommodate increasing amounts of the soul's energy.

Energy

Moving stuck energy gives us access to more energy. I mentioned previously, in this book, that the earth's energy is steadily increasing. It is transferring some of this energy to our bodies. We can utilize the energy best if our own energy systems are moving. In that case, the increase in energy will enhance our youthfulness, healing, well-being, and consciousness. If, however, there are places in the body where our energy is stuck, the increase in energy will exacerbate problems that are already there. It can register as pain, emotional ups and downs, mental problems, lethargy, anger or dis-ease. It can feel like the flu.

> Moving stuck energy gives us access to more energy.

Have you sometimes felt achy with no fever, or had mysterious aches and pains where you never felt them before? Have you gone to the doctor with strange symptoms, and nothing "wrong" could be found? Have you felt "run down" for no apparent reason? These may be signs that your energy is stuck. If we pay attention to these signals, we can pinpoint the areas that need our attention, and heal them before they develop into an illness.

Get Out Of The Ruts

Moving stuck energy can get us out of the ruts that keep us from living our happiest and most fulfilled lives. One of the ruts that a person complains about most is his or her job. Many people hate Monday mornings. They live for the weekends. People who feel dissatisfied and frustrated by their work or busy schedules typically have energy stuck in the fifth chakra. Stuck energy there can cause a person to feel trapped, limited, out of sync, off-track, and hopeless. The way out of this rut is to heal whatever is keeping us from living life in alignment with the soul.

> Moving stuck energy can get us out of the ruts that keep us from living our happiest and most fulfilled lives.

The Function of the Fifth Chakra

The fifth, or throat, chakra encompasses the throat, mouth, jaw, shoulders, arms and hands. The fifth chakra is the portal through which the soul carries out its mission and purpose, speaks its truth, and does the things that give it satisfaction. These are the things that give us ultimate fulfillment. They are the ways that our souls express and manifest themselves in physicality.

> The fifth chakra is the portal through which the soul carries out its mission and purpose, speaks its truth, and does the things that give it satisfaction.

Each of us, in our creation, has a unique mission, purpose, and function on this earth. Each of us has a unique set of soul vibrations that we are here to radiate. Each of us has an inner truth that we are here to bring forth. Each of us has certain gifts and abilities that are to be used for the benefit of this creation and for our own edification. When the fifth chakra is open, we are able to freely emanate our souls' vibrations, speak our inner truth, use our gifts, and fulfill our souls' purpose. We are generally happy, fulfilled, and enthusiastic about life.

Stuck Energy in the Fifth Chakra

When the fifth portal to the soul is blocked by stuck energy, it becomes very difficult to carry out the life purpose of the soul. The fifth chakra works with the third chakra to carry out the soul's will, and with the fourth chakra to manifest the soul's essence. If any one of these chakras is blocked, closed, or malfunctioning due to stuck energy, the functioning of the other two is also diminished. Stuck energy in those chakras may cause us to hide our souls' vibrations, follow someone else's truth, bury our gifts, and turn our backs on the will of our Higher Selves and the divine plan for our lives. When this happens, we are miserable. We describe ourselves as being "stuck in a rut".

Blocked energy in the fifth chakra will result in our saying and doing things that are not in harmony with our inner truth. It may lead us to pursue careers and activities that do not utilize our natural gifts or portray our true selves. This can cause us to become frustrated with our jobs, feel unfulfilled and weighed down by the pressures of life, live our lives for others or feel overly responsible for them, and generally become unhappy with the ways our lives are going.

Unhappiness, depression, and the feeling of being trapped are some of the emotional symptoms of a closed fifth chakra. There are plenty of physical symptoms as well. Stuck energy in the throat chakra contributes to such physical ailments as tight or sore throats, TMJ, sore and stiff shoulders and necks, rotator cuff problems, tennis elbow, and carpal tunnel syndrome.

Almost every client I see for massage complains of having at least one of these symptoms. The blame is usually placed on something like whiplash, strain, repetitive motion injury, sitting at a computer, or sleeping "the wrong way". These can bring the problem to the surface to be experienced at the physical level. The root cause of the problem is usually much deeper and less obvious.

The root causes of stuck energy in the fifth chakra are the things that keep us from living life from the soul. They diminish our joy and close the fifth chakra. The lack of vital life energy to the fifth chakra then causes physical problems. Let us address some of the most common causes of stuck energy and pain in the fifth chakra. A list is provided in the box found on the next page. Following that is a description of each of these common causes of stuck energy.

Causes of Stuck Energy in the Fifth Chakra

- **Withholding Our Truth**
- **Limiting Beliefs**
- **Running in "Survival Mode"**
- **Filtering New Information**
- **Judgments of Right and Wrong**
- **Linear Thinking**
- **Stress**
- **Living for Others**
- **Submitting to the Ego**
- **Trying to Impress Others**
- **Fear of Being Different**

Withholding Our Truth

Speaking our truth is one of the main functions of the fifth chakra. We must speak our truth if we are to keep this chakra open and the energy flowing through it. Our truth proceeds from our essence. We each see things from a different perspective because our core soul energies are different.

A widespread practice in our society is to tell others what they want to hear or to "go along with the program" instead of speaking and acting on our truth. We do this in an attempt to look good in others' eyes, to keep the peace, or to keep from hurting others.

Most people don't realize that they hurt others when they're not being true to themselves. The anger that they hold by not being themselves comes out as resentment, resistance, rebellion, and rage—energies that can close their chakras and separate them from others. When we are true to ourselves, we are innately happy. When we are innately happy, we have no need to feel like we need to hurt another. There are no ulterior motives in our words and actions toward others. We are not responsible for others' reactions to our truth. We end up doing far more damage to others and ourselves by putting up a false façade and holding back on our truth.

We are also not "called" to convince others that our truth is better or more accurate than theirs is. Our truth is our truth. Their truth is their truth. No one has a corner on truth. It is up to each of us to discern our own truth.

> We are not "called" to convince others that our truth is better or more accurate than theirs is.

The mouth and throat are the avenues through which we speak our truth. Those who hold back on speaking their truth or merely reiterate the truth of another are likely candidates for mouth, jaw, teeth, tongue, and throat problems. My colds, for example, seemed to always begin with a sore throat. The number of sore throats I get have lessened as I have opened my fifth chakra through speaking my truth. Those who do speak and live their truth not only live healthier and happier lives, but also are an encouragement to others to do the same.

Limiting Beliefs

Because the throat chakra is the place through which we speak our truth, it is also the chakra in which we hold many of the beliefs about ourselves and life in general. Beliefs and truth are not the same thing. Beliefs are the mechanism through which we mentally bring order and structure to our lives. Beliefs can and should change as we gain new information and expand our awareness. Truth is the unique perspective one's

> Beliefs are the mechanism through which we mentally bring order and structure to our lives. Truth is the unique perspective one's soul brings to life.

soul brings to life. It encompasses the visual, lingual, and behavioral manifestations of one's soul essence.

For example, if kindness is a key aspect of Mary's soul essence, then her truth will reflect that. Speaking and living her truth means that her words and actions come from the perspective of kindness.

When our beliefs are not in alignment with our truth, there is a dissonance created which causes a disruption in the flow of energy. Our beliefs can sometimes give us a distorted or false concept of ourselves and our function in life. They can keep us from fulfilling important roles we are to play, fracturing our joy. In Mary's case, one of her functions in life is to demonstrate kindness to others. If she were taught from a young age that people would take advantage of her if she were too kind, then that belief is in conflict with her truth. It prevents her from fully experiencing the joy of her innate kindness.

When our beliefs are not in alignment with our truth, there is a dissonance created which causes a disruption in the flow of energy.

Edward, one of my clients, has the innate wisdom and compassion to be a great leader. But Edward would not allow himself to assume a leadership role because of his self-limiting beliefs. He believed he was not good enough to be a leader. He believed that he was too shy to lead people. He questioned his intelligence and constantly second-guessed his innate wisdom, believing that others were right and he was wrong. Edward had a pattern of settling for jobs and positions that did not suit him and then wondered why he didn't feel fulfilled. As Edward worked on revising his self-limiting beliefs, he was able to create a new vision for his life—a vision that was more in line with his gifts, abilities, and life's purpose.

Energy that is stuck in the fifth chakra is commonly related to beliefs about the following:

- **Perceived lack of talents, gifts, and abilities**
- **The over-importance or lack of importance of one's life relative to others**
- **What it means to be a "good person"**
- **The meaning of "success"**
- **Competing male and female roles**
- **Right versus wrong**
- **Self limitations**

Beliefs that limit us can prevent us from attaining new heights of awareness and experiencing new things. Old, outdated beliefs can limit our freedom and keep us caged. Our energy becomes stuck when we don't allow our beliefs to evolve or change with our soul. When our soul is ready to give us a new or different experience, our belief systems can sometimes get in the way, thus causing us to become stuck in the same old rut.

For example, when I left my engineering job to become a writer, many of my co-workers told me they wished they could make such a dramatic change in their lives. They were either not happy doing what they were doing, or felt they would be more fulfilled doing something else. Some were even feeling an inner tug to do something different.

What was stopping them from making this change? Partly it was their beliefs—beliefs about what it takes to be successful, what one must do to provide for one's family, and the "security" that a steady income provides.

These are the very things that I faced after I quit my job. My belief about the importance of having money to give me a sense of security came up as I saw my savings go down to zero. My belief about being a good mother surfaced as I saw my kids scraping to financially make it through college. Although I helped them as much as I could, I wanted to do more. My belief about the definition of success emerged as I gave up my title and comfortable income.

But every time those old beliefs came up, I asked myself, "What is my *soul* wanting to do? What is it showing me through this change? What is most important in my life?" Gradually the old beliefs were replaced by new ones, which are more aligned with my soul's truth and purpose. I have more joy now, and feel more fulfilled and complete than I ever did under my old belief structure and way of living. As I live in the authenticity of my soul, my energy flows. I don't worry about money. There has always been enough. Here are some of the new beliefs that replaced those which no longer served me:

- **Success is living each day in the integrity of my soul.**
- **True joy comes from living my truth.**
- **Abundance is a state of being.**
- **Life is not about doing what is "right"; it is about *being* fully who I am.**
- **The most important role I have as a mother is to accept my children as they are and help them to love themselves.**

Are you currently feeling like something is keeping you from making a needed change in your life? Ground yourself and ask your Higher Self to reveal to you any beliefs that might be holding you back. Then ask your Higher Self to replace those beliefs, all the way down to the DNA level, with those that are in alignment with your truth at this time. Write down the new beliefs given to you by your Higher Self and repeat them often to yourself.

Running in "Survival Mode"

A large portion of humanity believes that their main occupation in life is to survive. They may not express that belief in those exact words. But they work two and three jobs, take on overtime, and obsess over having enough money in order to keep food on the table, clothes on their backs, and a shelter over their heads. Our world and most of its societies have been structured to support that belief—to keep people so focused on surviving that they have no time for the really important things in life, such as family nurturing, self-fulfillment, and healing.

And yet the reality is, there is enough money in the world. If it were to be distributed equally, every single adult and child would be a millionaire! Who is benefiting from this disparity? It certainly is not the major population of the world. If we are to change the current state of affairs, we must change our beliefs about survival. Our thoughts and beliefs create our reality.

Drawing our physical needs to us is the job of the first chakra. Our fears of not having enough and our belief that we must work hard to survive have prevented the first chakra from doing its job. It was mentioned in Portal #1 that we are to set our intentions and needs in our energy field and then trust and allow the Universe to draw them to us through the first chakra.

Instead, we have been using our fifth chakra to manifest our needs. We have been focusing the energy of this chakra toward work that is not fulfilling—toward work that merely allows us to survive. This is a misuse of the fifth chakra, and it causes energy to become stuck there. It uses much more energy than is really needed to survive. We must let the first chakra do its job and supply us with what we need to live a physical life. Then we can use the fifth chakra for its intended purpose: to speak and live our truth and bring fulfillment to the soul.

It's no wonder that so many people have pain in their hands, arms, shoulders, and necks. They are working too hard. One wouldn't use a hammer to drive a screw. It not only takes much more energy; it also damages the screw and the wood, producing holes, splinters, stripped threads, and a weakened connection. Using our chakras for something other than their intended purposes reduces their energy, function, and connection to the earth, soul, and Universe. If the first and fifth chakras are encouraged to perform their functions, then they can work together in harmony and ease to bring us abundance *and* do the activities that give us the most joy. It is time to stop working so hard at living and really live!

Filtering New Information

The throat chakra holds beliefs that act as filters to new information. These beliefs can help us to be discerning if they are in alignment with our souls' truth and essence, and work in conjunction with the wisdom of our Higher Selves. They can also make us close-minded if they prevent us from knowing and expanding our truth and awareness.

For example, if a woman believes that western medicine has the only valid approach to healing her illness, she will not be open to alternative healing therapies, even if western medicine has not provided a solution to her problem. If a man believes that his lot in life is to be in pain, he will not investigate new ways to heal the pain.

There is a great deal of new information coming forth at this time. We must rely on our inner wisdom to help discern what works for us. We will find much of the new information to be very helpful if we don't automatically discount its validity because it does not fit into our old belief structures.

One of the most prevalent filtering beliefs held in the throat chakra is that new information cannot come from within us—that it must come from another source. This is a filter that keeps us from bringing forth our truth to the world. Each one of our souls is an expert on *something*. We each have information to bring to the world. It is part of our truth. Some may understand how to better bring forth a person's gifts and essence through parenting or teaching. Others may assist governments and institutions in finding new paradigms of coexistence and collaborative leadership. Some may develop new healing methods and technologies. Others may create healthier ways to grow and prepare food. Some may have insights on how to clean up the environment. Others may have ways to support symbiosis between the earth and the life that dwells on it.

> One of the most prevalent filtering beliefs held in the throat chakra is that new information cannot come from within us—that it must come from another source.

Being open to and trusting the information that is within us, and being willing to share that information with others, is key to opening the fifth chakra and accomplishing our own life's purpose. People who depend solely on the information that comes from others, and don't listen to their own inner wisdom, suppress their truth and may consequently feel stuck.

This book is a good example of that. I knew from the get-go that this book was a portrayal of my own healing process. What I didn't know, until I was almost finished with the first draft, was that it was a book about healing the chakras. I hadn't realized, until that point, that my own healing process had been a steady progression that addressed each chakra in order from the first to the seventh. When I came to that realization, I spent days researching and compiling information, already written on the chakras, to include in this book.

After the research was completed, some of the information that I had compiled didn't quite fit with my own experience of the chakras. I struggled internally over how to make the old information fit into my experience. The writing that had flowed so easily came to a grinding halt. I was stuck. At that point, my Higher Self told me to ignore what had previously been written and allow myself to bring forth a fresh perspective.

That did not make the traditional information "wrong". It simply added to it, completing more of the overall picture regarding the chakras. This book was not to be a rewrite of what had already been done. Rather, it was to be an enhancement of it, based on the truth that my soul is here to bring forth to benefit the global society in which I live. Each of us has information and truth to contribute. When our individual knowledge and perceptions are combined, a more complete picture comes forth for humankind.

When our individual knowledge and perceptions are combined, a more complete picture comes forth for humankind.

Right and Wrong

A belief that is related to the belief of having to rely on others for information is that there is a right and a wrong way of doing things. The mind likes to dwell on absolutes. The soul is much more flexible. It prefers to try new ways of doing things. This is a form of play for the soul. If given the freedom to do so, it will create new ways of doing things that are more in alignment with the soul and the current way of life than are the "tried and true" methods already developed. Allowing the soul the flexibility to be different and try new approaches helps to open the fifth chakra.

The belief that there is "one best way" of doing something brings the energy of rigidity into the neck and shoulder area. It can be felt as tightness in the neck. This perfectionist, right and wrong, way of thinking can pervade every facet of our lives. It can affect our ideas and beliefs on such things as: romance, relationship, parenting, education, work, career, religion, spirituality, physical appearance, wellness, diet, and much, much more. What is right for one may not work for another. It may not be the experience that the soul desires to have. This "right and wrong" type of thinking causes separation. In the extreme, it has been the basis for religious wars, attacks at abortion clinics, and splits within churches. In our daily lives, believing that there is only one way to approach an aspect of our lives is a rut to our growth and evolution and a despoiler of unity.

In our daily lives, believing that there is only one way to approach an aspect of our lives is a rut to our growth and evolution and a despoiler of unity.

Linear Thinking

When we focus very narrowly on a particular goal, idea, or way of doing something, we put ourselves in the mode of linear thinking. We become like trail horses that won't stray off the path, even though the view in front of them is another horse's derrière. Having goals is not the problem. Goals help us to get things done. The problem lies in being so attached to our goals that we do not allow our souls the flexibility to change direction.

The muscles in the neck can be compared to the reins on a horse. They cause the head to move in various directions. The SCM muscles on either side of the head rotate the head to the right and left. Other neck muscles tilt the head forward and backward. These muscles are tight, and usually painful, in almost every client that comes to me for massage. I am convinced that one reason for this is that we are at a point in our evolution where we are being called to release our linear, goal-oriented, way of thinking and "go with the flow".

If the reins are dropped on a horse, the horse may then go in any direction it wishes, at any speed it desires. If we will let go of our rigid ideas of how life "should be", and release our attachment to our goals, we will give ourselves free rein to follow the direction of our souls. Going with the flow of the moment, instead of insisting that we follow a linear path, should release much of the tension in our necks. Although linear thinking has served us in many ways in the past, it is currently a rut to our evolution, freedom, and the shear joy of living. It limits the function of, and flow of energy in, the higher chakras.

Stress

Stress is another source of stuck energy and tightness in the neck and shoulders. Most of the stress in our lives is self-induced. We set unreal expectations of ourselves, trying to accomplish too much in too little time. We prevent ourselves from going with the flow by packing our agendas full of deadlines and activities. This leaves very little room for spontaneity and causes us to feel overwhelmed.

We also allow others to transfer their tension and stress onto us. The deadlines of our customers become our deadlines. The frenetic pace of our bosses becomes our pace. The worries and priorities of our parents, children, partners, and friends become our worries and priorities. Tension breeds tension. It literally becomes a "pain in the neck" as the reins upon us grow tighter and tighter, both from within and from without.

Living for Others

One of the causes of these tight reigns is a distorted sense of responsibility. Some people feel that they are responsible for the happiness of others, especially those they love. We are to treat one another with honor and respect. Parents are responsible for the safety and well-being of their minor children. But we are not responsible for another's happiness. That is something that each of us must achieve on our own. To bypass one's own happiness for the happiness of another is a transgression against one's soul. It causes a person to feel weighed down and joyless.

> We are not responsible for another's happiness.

I am not speaking of the loving assistance we give to others. I am referring to the almost slave-like abandonment of one's life for another. Feeling overly responsible for others is like having a yoke, upon one's shoulders, containing a burden too great to bear. This yoke creates soreness at the base of the neck down into the shoulders. Some people live their lives for others out of obligation and guilt. Others allow people to bully or manipulate them into meeting their demands. Living like this closes the fifth chakra.

We would do well to keep in mind that we are not responsible for the choices and decisions that others make. It is tempting to want to rescue people from the choices they have made. But we could spend our whole lives doing just that. It is very difficult to live our own lives when we are constantly assisting others in carrying out the decisions they have made or getting them out of the messes they have created. Living for others causes our energy to become stuck. It does not bring joy or fulfillment to the soul. It leads to a hollow and depleted existence, free of the passion, freedom, and fulfillment that we are meant to have.

Submitting to the Ego

Living our lives for others' purposes is one rut that keeps us from fulfilling our own soul's purpose. Living our lives according to the demands of our own ego, and not following the leading of our soul and Higher Self, is another.

If the ego's agenda is not in alignment with the soul's essence and purpose or the agenda of the Higher Self, a conflict can develop between the mind (representing the ego) and the heart (representing the soul). Since the throat chakra is the energetic connection between the head and the heart, the conflict tends to manifest itself in the fifth chakra. Stuck energy there may cause us to say and do things that do not represent our true selves. We may wonder why our actions aren't consistent, why we say things that we don't mean, why we chose a career or job that we don't enjoy, or why we are too busy to enjoy our lives.

Consulting our Higher Selves regarding our priorities and activities can prevent these problems and ameliorate the tension and stress that are created by a too-busy life style. Many of the activities we commit to and do are not necessarily in alignment with the divine plan for our lives. If that is the case, they neither give us joy in doing them, nor do they serve the best and highest good. We can change this by asking our Higher Selves to set our priorities and by consulting our Higher Selves about our activities each day. This helps to open the fifth chakra and create a life that flows with ease and joy.

If the things we do in life are out of alignment with the soul's essence and the divine plan for our lives, there will be a tendency to feel stuck, trapped, and resentful. There may also be feelings of needing to work very hard to get anything accomplished, having to do it all alone, or forcing the situation.

If the things we do in life are out of alignment with the soul's essence and the divine plan for our lives, there will be a tendency to feel stuck, trapped, and resentful.

It is possible to mistake the urges of the ego for the desires of the soul. You will learn how to tell the difference between the ego's insistent urgings and the soul's gentle promptings in the Seventh Portal. A dissonance between our activities and the divine plan for our lives will oftentimes be accompanied by physical pain somewhere in the fifth chakra. The pain frequently shows up between the shoulders and hands. Just as the throat and mouth are the verbal expression of our being, the hands, arms, and shoulders are the "doing" aspect of it.

A dissonance between our activities and the divine plan for our lives will oftentimes be accompanied by physical pain somewhere in the fifth chakra.

There are minor chakras in the palms of the hands. When what we do in our daily lives does not represent who we are, and is not in alignment with the divine plan for our lives, the hand chakras close down. When these chakras are closed, energy backs up into the hands, wrists, elbows, arms, and shoulders, leading to such things as numbness, rotator cuff problems, tennis elbow, and carpal tunnel syndrome.

As is true of all the chakras, the *intention* to open the hand chakras is the key to opening them. I use a circular motion with the fingers of the opposing hand to open the chakra at the palm. The hands may also be clapped or rubbed together in a circular motion. *Keeping* them open, however, will only happen if the stuck energies, or issues, that are preventing us from living our truth, are addressed. The ego is oftentimes at fault. It may cause us to have distorted beliefs about what is important and worthwhile in life. It may have a false perception of self, a resistance to change, and a lack of balance and integration in one's masculine and feminine sides. It may operate from feelings of guilt, obligation, or the need to impress others.

Trying to Impress Others

The gap between the person that the ego projects to the world and the real true self can be broad and devastating. It not only causes energy to become stuck in the fifth chakra, but also can be toxic to the soul. You will learn how to bridge this gap to live your life in alignment with your soul in the second book of this series. One thing we must always remember is: There is nothing to prove. There is only experience.

> There is nothing to prove.
> There is only experience.

Trying to impress others with our knowledge, abilities, success, possessions, activities, or goodness actually puts us in a position of inferiority. It opens us up to their judgment. It is impossible to meet the expectations of everyone around us. Besides, meeting the expectations of others is not the way to avoid judgment. We will continue to draw people into our lives that judge us in the same ways that we judge ourselves. We avoid judgment by being ourselves and not judging who we are, living life in accordance with our soul, and accepting that everything we have done is part of the rich experience of this life. When we stop trying to impress others, we give ourselves the freedom to be who we are. It is an opening to the soul.

Fear of Being Different

The fear of being different, of not fitting in, or not being accepted, is an energy that is commonly stuck in the fifth chakra. This fear keeps us from living our truth. We were not created to be carbon copies of one another. We were born as individuals, with unique gifts, abilities, and vibrations. We were meant to combine these unique qualities for the best and highest good of all. That is where the joy is. Being ourselves—speaking and living our truth—is an essential part of living a happy, fulfilled, honest, and free existence. Trying to be like everyone else only serves those whose intention is to control us.

Stuck Energy in the Other Chakras

Stuck energy in the fifth chakra puts us in a rut of self-denial. Stuck energy in the other six chakras puts us in other kinds of ruts. Do you find it difficult to support yourself? Have you been unable to find "true love"? Do you unconsciously sabotage your life? Are you being controlled by those around you? Do you wish you could connect with your Higher Self, see things from the soul's perspective, and receive accurate guidance?

These are all symptoms of stuck energy in one or more chakras. We have addressed some of the origins of stuck energy in the fifth chakra. These, and other causes, can contribute to stuck energy and problems in the other chakras as well. Some of them are listed in the box below.

Causes of Stuck Energy

- **Trauma**
- **Abuse**
- **Control**
- **Attachments**
- **Pent-up Emotions**
- **Guilt and Shame**
- **Resentment**
- **Fear**
- **Limiting Beliefs**
- **Judgment**
- **Defense Mechanisms**
- **Unresolved Karma**
- **Toxicity**

Coming to awareness of the things that cause our energy to slow down is the first step toward getting it to move again. We will take a brief look at each of the above causes of stuck energy to enhance your awareness of their effects on you. You will then be given some ways to move your energy so you can get out of the ruts that are caused by stuck energy.

Physical Trauma

Physical trauma can affect any of the chakras. Most of us have undergone some kind of physical trauma—a fall, a car or bicycle accident, or surgery, for example. Any kind of trauma to the physical body can disrupt the flow of energy. The memory of the trauma becomes stuck in the cells of the immediate and adjoining tissues and becomes a sinkhole for energy. That is one reason why, after an injury or surgery, it is so important to do things to keep the energy moving—walk, do yoga, get a massage or chiropractic adjustment, have acupuncture, do energy work, etc. It helps the body to release the cellular memory of the trauma so that the body can heal.

Physical trauma causes energy to slow down in the physical body. The root cause of the trauma, however, can be hidden from sight. It is my belief that most, if not all, of our physical trauma is precipitated by karma or some underlying issue. I don't believe in "accidents". If there are unresolved issues corrupting our DNA or slowing down the energy in our etheric body, I believe that they will eventually manifest as an illness or injury to the correlating part of our physical body. If we don't address the problem in its early manifestations, it is likely to get worse and worse. It is important to pay attention to the

> It is important to pay attention to the things that happen to our bodies and the signals that they give us. They are clues that can help us acknowledge and heal our internal issues.

things that happen to our bodies and the signals that they give us. They are clues that can help us acknowledge and heal our internal issues.

Abuse

Abuse, that has not been forgiven, is one of the underlying causes of stuck energy. Sexual and emotional abuse and issues related to one's sexuality are likely to slow down the movement of energy in the second chakra (encompassing the abdomen and sexual organs). This may show up as abuse of others, cancer, fibroids, cysts, blood clots, organ malfunction, or the inability to become intimate. Moving the energy in the second chakra can relieve physical problems in that area, including some of the symptoms of menopause and PMS. Much of this stuck energy can be healed with forgiveness.

Control

Abuse, which normally affects the second chakra, can have its origin in the third chakra with issues of control. Trying to control or, alternatively, giving up one's power, may be due to the presence of thought forms and beliefs about hierarchy and competition: that one person is better than another, is more worthy or more deserving. The "undeserving" end up being controlled and oftentimes abused.

The belief that people should be controlled is pervasive in our society and our world. It is the basic premise behind the working structure of many of our governments, religions, corporations, institutions, and relationships. It is one of the most limiting beliefs that we have, and causes our very lives and souls to be controlled by forces outside ourselves. For example:

The belief that people should be controlled is pervasive in our society and our world.

Sally was taught from childhood that a "good" woman must be submissive to her husband. Sally is finding that the decrees of her husband are far from fulfilling. She is at a point where she is ready to take charge of her own life. Her belief system will not allow her to do so. She is stuck in a passionless existence, and having all kinds of third chakra physical problems as well (problems with the stomach, small intestine, gall bladder, and liver). It is time for the old belief to be replaced by one that better serves her. It could be something like, "I know what is best for me", or "I am responsible for my life", or "I am an equal partner in this relationship".

Control slows down our energy dramatically. Freeing ourselves to live in the personal sovereignty of our souls' wills, beyond control, allows us to soar with our souls to enjoy lives of freedom and fulfillment.

Attachments

Attachments to things, people, and ideas slow down our energy. Attachments to things are found in the first chakra. Hoarding money, stockpiling, or hanging on to possessions that are no longer used are all signs of attachments to things. They can prevent the easy flow of abundance through our lives. The belief that one must have certain material things to be happy or successful can lead to an attachment to those things, causing undue stress and financial problems in trying to acquire them.

Attachments to people are located in the second and third chakras. They can cause us to be overly protective of others for fear of losing them. They can also cause us to hold on to our parents, children, romantic partners, or friends in an unhealthy or controlling way, limiting their freedom.

Attachments to beliefs and ideas are primarily found in the fifth and sixth chakras. These cause us to dismiss new ideas or the input of others. They cause us to be rigid in our thinking and approach to life. Many of our attachments have to do with a belief that things must be a certain way. "I will finally be fulfilled when..."; or "My happiness depends upon..."; or "My ideal mate will look like..." are examples of attachments. They are often so subtle that we don't even realize we have them.

For example, Martha might tell Jonathon that she loves him. Perhaps, underneath those words, she is really saying, "I expect you to act in certain ways to make me feel loved." Or she might be saying, "I am looking to you to fulfill my hopes and dreams of home, family, security, and happiness."

While these may all be good things, they are still expectations based upon attachment. They have little to do with pure love. Martha might even try controlling the relationship to get what she wants. Love with attachments such as these can put the relationship in a rut, setting it up for disappointment or failure. It limits the flow of energy between the romantic partners.

Pure love, without attachment, desires the highest good of all. It allows both parties to fully be themselves—an important aspect of keeping one's energy moving. Allowing things, people, and ideas to flow freely in and out of our lives reduces our stress, disappointment, and anguish, and keeps our energy moving.

Allowing things, people, and ideas to flow freely in and out of our lives reduces our stress, disappointment, and anguish, and keeps our energy moving.

Pent-up Emotions

Energy can become stuck due to pent-up emotions and emotional trauma, just as it does with physical trauma. It is important to feel our emotions and allow the energy of them to move through us. This can be done by acknowledging and breathing through our emotions as they arise.

Unfortunately, we have been trained to do just the opposite. We have been conditioned to think that our emotions are bad or embarrassing. We've been told, "Don't cry"; "Don't get angry"; "Don't be so emotional"; and "Get over it!" We have been ridiculed, punished, and made to feel guilty and shameful for showing our emotions. So we hold our breath, stuff our emotions back into our bodies and then, years later, feel the mental and physical effects of all those emotions that have never been expressed. Chronic problems in any of the first five chakras can be the result of unexpressed emotions. Forgiveness and the Emotional Freedom Technique (E.F.T.) can be used to heal traumatic memories, phobias, guilt, grief, and physical ailments. E.F.T. is an emotional form of acupuncture in which the fingertips are used to tap and stimulate certain meridian energy points to move stuck energy. [1]

Guilt and Shame

There are several emotions that are so devastating to the flow of our energy, that it is worthwhile making special mention of them. They are holding tanks for stuck energy. Guilt and shame are two of them. They have been used to control us by making us feel substandard, inferior, wrong, or unworthy.

When we don't measure up to outside expectations, or when we make decisions that others consider "wrong", guilt and shame are heaped upon us. It is time to let go of that. It is not up to anyone else to tell us that we are wrong. They can tell us how they feel, but it is not their responsibility to judge us.

> Hanging on to guilt and shame over something we have done keeps that memory locked in our system and blocks our energy.

[1] For information on E.F.T., visit the www.emofree.com website.

Likewise, we should not judge ourselves. We learn by experience, and we are free to choose differently next time. Hanging on to guilt and shame over something we have done keeps that memory locked in our system and blocks our energy It prevents us from evolving. Guilt and shame, which primarily affect chakras two through five, are healed with forgiveness.

Resentment

Resentment, sometimes called unforgiveness, is another emotion that is a holding tank for stuck energy. When we hang on to the memories of ways we have been "wronged" by others, we do not allow ourselves to learn the lessons they were teaching us by their actions.

> When we hang on to the memories of ways we have been "wronged" by others, we do not allow ourselves to learn the lessons they were teaching us by their actions.

People mirror for us what is inside us. If there is something about ourselves that we don't accept, we will draw people to us that bring it to our attention. For example, if Margie unconsciously feels she doesn't deserve to be loved, she will quite likely enter into abusive or unloving relationships. As we learn to love ourselves, we tend to bring loving people into our lives.

Resentment can be stored in any of the first five chakras. It is healed with forgiveness. Forgiveness not only gets our own energy moving again, but it also releases those we've harbored resentment against to heal and move forward.

Fear

We addressed fear in the last chapter. Fear is an emotion that slows down and contracts our energy into dense pockets. What kinds of fears are you aware of having? Most of us are well aware of fears we may have of spiders, snakes, heights, flying, speaking in public, etc. We learn to accept these things about ourselves and work around them, or get help to work through them. But there are many more fears, that lie beneath our conscious awareness, that can have an even stronger effect on us and our lives than the fears we know about. Such was the case with Kathy, who was one of my regular massage clients.

Kathy came to me complaining of lower back pain. She had a knot on the left side of her lower back the size of a golf ball. She had been to various doctors about it, but they could find no cause for it. I tried several massage techniques to reduce the size of the knot and relieve her pain, but nothing worked.

Finally, after a month of weekly massage, I suggested that she come in for an intuitive session to find out what might be causing the knot in her lower back to be so stubborn. The week prior to the session, her back pain grew worse and the knot grew bigger than ever, which is a common sign that it is time for healing.

During the session, we asked Kathy's Higher Self to show her what was causing the knot to form. Several fears came to her awareness as we worked. Kathy became aware of a fear of following her soul's leading in decision making. Her mind and ego insisted on being in control. She was afraid that she would lose everything and not be able to support herself. I explained to Kathy that the mind and ego are meant to work with the soul, not in competition with it. She was able to heal the fear with forgiveness. The golf-ball sized lump immediately decreased in size. As one fear after another was healed, the lump became smaller and smaller, and the pain went away.

In my practice, I frequently see things like this happen. Energy that has become stuck through fear, stuffed emotions, abuse, etc. ends up manifesting itself through physical problems. When the issues are brought to one's conscious awareness and healed, it allows the energy to move again, and the body heals. In Kathy's case, the fears were lodged in the cellular memory, meridians, and gridwork of her lower back, causing the energy there to build up and form a lump. The size of the lump decreased as the fears and stuck energy were released. This can be an iterative process, where layers come off over time, causing the pain to occasionally resurface so that more healing can occur at a deeper level. This is exactly what happened with Kathy.

A couple of weeks later, the knot had again grown, and the pain returned. More intuitive work revealed another layer of fears to be released. These had to do with intimacy and setting boundaries in her relationships. As these were acknowledged and healed, the knot grew smaller and the pain diminished.

Soon after these sessions, Kathy was guided to increase the size of her business. She proceeded to do so without reservation. Problems in a close relationship were also being resolved as she took charge of setting her boundaries. Releasing her fears had helped her to get on with her life and make it more joyful and prosperous.

Fear can be found in any of the chakras. Fears of not having enough, contracting a serious illness, not being safe, or dying are located in the first chakra. Fears of separation and intimacy become lodged in the second chakra. Fears of authority and making the wrong decision are held in the third chakra. Fears of being hurt emotionally produce the defense mechanisms in the fourth chakra. Fears of not fitting in or not doing the "right" thing reside in the fifth chakra. These fears can cause a multitude of physical, mental, and emotional problems. There are even fears of being too beautiful, too rich, too powerful, and too successful. They keep us stuck in a rut of feeling inferior, preventing us from living the joyful and fulfilled lives that come from soaring with our souls. Speaking or writing our fears, as Kathy did, helps to bring them to the surface so that the stuck energy and behavior patterns can be healed.

Limiting Beliefs

We have already addressed some of the limiting beliefs that become stuck in the fifth chakra. Limiting beliefs can be found in any of the chakras. They are related to, and therefore limit, the function of the chakra to which they are attached. An example of a limiting belief in the first chakra would be, "I do not deserve to have abundance."

Limiting beliefs put us in ruts that keep us from living our most joyful, productive, aware, and powerful lives. What are your current beliefs about money, security, relationship, sex, personal sovereignty, love, happiness, work, success, and spirituality? Are any of them starting to feel like a limitation to you? How might they be changed to reflect more accurately the person that *you* are?

You can ask your Higher Self to help you revise your beliefs so that they align more closely with your soul. We would do well to constantly monitor our belief systems and replace any that no longer serve our highest good or the highest good of all.

You can ask your Higher Self to help you revise your beliefs so that they align more closely with your soul.

Judgment

Our belief systems can lead us into judgment. Judgments polarize and separate people, causing stuck energy in the fourth chakra. They come forth as prejudice, discrimination, fanaticism, chauvinism, bigotry, etc. These judgments contract the heart energy. "We are right and they are wrong"; or "Our ways are good, and theirs are bad"; or "We are better than they" are examples of such judgments.

There is a vast difference between discerning what is appropriate for ourselves and making sweeping statements about what is "right" for all people. Global judgments like that stem from a singular perspective. They lack compassion and acceptance, and foster separation. They slow down our energy and that of the world around us.

Defense Mechanisms

While we are focusing on the heart, let us consider our defense mechanisms. These mechanisms act as shields around the heart chakra. Defense mechanisms do not allow the energy to flow freely between two people. They destroy trust. Stuck energy around the heart can lead to heart disease, pressure and pain in the heart area, clogged blood vessels, and lung disease.

Just before I began to clear what was causing the energy to stagnate around my own heart, I began to experience pain around my heart and down my left arm. A stress test indicated that my heart was in perfect shape. Emotionally, it felt like a black, bottomless well, full of sadness and tears.

As I have cleared my own defense mechanisms, healed what was behind them, and opened up my heart chakra, the bottomless well has become a spring of love flowing to myself and those around me. The emotional emptiness and physical pain are gone. It has been replaced by an indescribable sense of fullness and well-being.

Unresolved Karma

The causes of stuck energy that we have discussed so far can have their roots in unresolved karma. Karma may lie beneath our injuries, pent-up emotions, fears, abusive encounters, control issues, limiting belief systems, judgments, attachments, and defense mechanisms. Karma can cause energy to become stuck anywhere in the physical body, chakras, and etheric body.

Our physical symptoms and injuries are very good indicators of where we might have unresolved karma to be addressed. Even such things as a broken bone or the loss of a limb can be the result of unresolved karma. Our thoughts and emotions can also point to the source of the karma.

It is always best to ask one's Higher Self for input when resolving our karma. The Higher Self can shed a great deal of light on why the karma is there. This can facilitate the healing of the karma, as the following example illustrates.

Maddie came to me with tenderness in the area of her solar plexus, along with frequent upset stomachs. These physical problems pointed to the third chakra as the location of her stuck energy. When we asked her Higher Self to inform us regarding what was stuck there, she began to feel very sad. We asked her Higher Self what was the source of Maddie's sadness.

Maddie was shown that she had relinquished her sovereignty to others. In their codependent relationship, her husband used his disapproval and disappointment to get her to do what he wanted. The sadness was coming directly from her soul as she compromised her soul's will for that of her husband's. Upon further reflection, Maddie realized that most of her close relationships were based upon this same pattern. She consistently did what her parents, friends, and children expected of her in order to please them and to feel good about herself. Underneath, she was not feeling good about herself at all.

Maddie was shown that this was a karmic issue that she had had for a very long time. It stemmed from a time when she had used anger and disapproval to control others. The karma, stuck energy, and behavior patterns were healed with the vibration of forgiveness, allowing Maddie to take charge of her own life. Whenever an issue comes to our awareness to be healed, it is a good idea to release any karma that may be behind it.

Toxicity

Excess toxins in our bodies slow down our energy. They cause our cells and systems to work inefficiently. This prevents our bodies from keeping pace vibrationally with our souls. It also causes all kinds of pain and health-related issues. I can always tell when I am overly toxic, because my thighs ache, my legs can't be still, and I get headaches.

Most of us have stored toxins in our bodies from the contaminants in our water, air, food, and the various products that we use. As we move and increase our energy, the stored toxins are released. Drinking a minimum of 6-8 glasses of pure water daily is essential for keeping the body hydrated and flushing out toxins. We should make every attempt to reduce the amount of toxins we take in, as well as detoxify on a regular basis. There are many products, techniques, and cleansing fasts available to help us detoxify the body. It is also a good idea to detoxify the aura. Epson salt or sea salt baths, after-shower salt scrubs, and exposure to the sun during the less intense hours of the day are all good aura cleansers.

All of the foregoing discussion regarding causes of stuck energy demonstrates that there are many things that can slow down our energy. These can cause us to feel stuck in emotional and mental ruts, to become sick, and to age as our cells decay. But there are also many ways to open the energy back up and get it moving again. We do have a choice!

How to Move Stuck Energy

You have already learned, in this book, several ways to move stuck energy. You learned how to stay grounded in Portal #1. Staying grounded is an important factor in moving stuck energy. Our bodies are similar to the cars we drive in that respect. If the battery is not grounded, its energy cannot flow through the systems of the car. It won't even start. We too must stay grounded in order for our energy to flow properly.

In Portal #2, you learned how to use your powers of observation to discern what your soul is trying to teach you. This is how you discover and uncover the emotional blockages, fears, belief systems, attachments, defense mechanisms, and karma that are keeping your energy stuck and preventing you from fully being yourself.

You then learned how to resolve your karma through forgiveness in Portal #3. You also used forgiveness, in Portal #4, to heal stuck memories and situations from your past, bringing you back to your center. Forgiveness can be used to heal many of the causes of stuck energy that we have addressed in this chapter.

You then learned, in Portal #4, how to move through your fears and anxieties of the future by using the vibration of surrender, helping you to free yourself of these immobilizing conditions. You learned in that same chapter how to do a breathing exercise that enhances the movement of your chi to move through stuck energy. So, you see, you already have many tools at your disposal for moving stuck energy, getting out of the ruts that it causes, and healing yourself.

As we clear out the stuck emotions, attachments, karma, and thought forms that no longer serve us, we actually increase our energy. This begins a wonderful upward spiral of healing and evolution. As our vibration rises, it brings that which no longer serves us to the surface to be acknowledged and healed. That increases our vibration further, thus bringing the next layer of stuck energy to the surface to be healed. It is a continuous process.

The sequencing of the chapters in this book was designed to help you systematically raise your vibration. It goes through the chakras from the first to the seventh. Of those seven chakras, the first chakra vibrates at the lowest frequency, while the seventh chakra vibrates at the highest frequency.

The sequencing of the chapters in this book was designed to help you systematically raise your vibration.

You may have discovered by now that, when you begin to open the next higher chakra, more issues, stuck energy, and its accompanying aches and pains, are brought to the surface in the lower vibrational chakras. These are the deeper issues and related stuck energy of those chakras. It sometimes takes a higher vibration to bring them to the surface. It is important to take the time to address and work with those deeper issues as part of the overall healing process. It is not something about which to become discouraged. It is a natural occurrence. We didn't get to the state of density and decay we are in overnight. We must be patient, and allow ourselves the time it takes to rise out of it.

We didn't get to the state of density and decay we are in overnight. We must be patient, and allow ourselves the time it takes to rise out of it.

When you are experiencing physical problems, be sure to ask your Higher Self whether or not there are issues beneath them to be addressed. Your Higher Self will usually bring something to your awareness. There may be times when your Higher Self tells you that the issues have already been addressed. In that case, the aches and pains are the result of the body's healing process as you raise your vibration further. If, however, you are having chronic problems and not getting any answers from your Higher Self, you may want to consult with an intuitive practitioner to help you discover what is beneath them. Sometimes we block our own healing process, and it becomes difficult to get answers to certain questions. The reasons for that, along with the way to work with one's soul to remove the blocks, will be addressed in the second book of this series.

Mind-Body Practices for Moving Stuck Energy

The body has many of its own natural ways of moving energy. These include the body's natural rhythms and mechanics. The breath, blood, lymph, cerebro-spinal fluid, and digestive and urinary tracts each have their own unique rhythm and pumping mechanism. They move energy as they transfer nutrients, oxygen, hormones, toxins, and wastes, among other things, in and out of the cells, organs, and body. The body's reproductive system moves sexual energy for both pleasure and healing through the movements and contractions associated with arousal and orgasm. The release of body fluids during sex, menstruation, coughing, sneezing, sinus drainage, and crying help the body to move energy and release toxins and stuck energy. Muscle ticks, spasms, cramps, jerks, shaking, etc. are ways that the body moves energy through involuntary muscle movement.

There are many things we can do to assist the body. The mind-body practices in this section aid and amplify the body's ability to move energy in a number of ways. Some are done alone, and others with the assistance of a facilitator or practitioner. Some are spiritual; others are physical; still others are emotional or mental; and some are a combination of these.

> Anything we do to move our energy is beneficial to all parts of our being, impacting our sense of well-being and connectedness, our health, creativity, and evolution.

When the energy of any part of us becomes stuck (physical, mental, emotional, or spiritual), it slows down the energies of the other parts of us, and affects how we feel and function. Likewise, when the energy of a particular aspect of ourselves begins to move, it helps to free up the energies of the other aspects. So anything we do to move our energy is beneficial to all parts of our being, impacting our sense of well-being and connectedness, our health, creativity, and evolution.

Listed on the following page are some of the many ways to move stuck energy. Ask your Higher Self to reveal to you the ways that work best for you, or simply do what you enjoy. There is an excellent book that explains many of the mind-body practices that can relieve pain, reduce stress, and foster health, spiritual growth, and inner peace. It is called *Discovering the Body's Wisdom*, by Mirka Knaster.[2] Most of the modalities listed below are explained in that book.

Many of these modalities fall under the categories of massage and bodywork, defined as "the application of systematic touch for health purposes".[3] The definitions of the various types of massage and bodywork modalities, along with the names and locations of local practitioners, may be found on the Internet.[4] Energetic DNA healing is a relatively new modality that can be very effective in moving stuck energy and healing physical, mental, emotional, and spiritual problems. Information and practitioners can be found by doing a search on the Internet or by visiting the bridgesofunity.com website.

Energetic DNA healing is a relatively new modality that can be very effective in moving stuck energy and healing physical, mental, emotional, and spiritual problems.

[2] Mirka Knaster, *Discovering the Body's Wisdom* (New York: Bantam Books, 1996).

[3] Sandy Fritz, *Mosby's Fundamentals of Therapeutic Massage* (St. Louis, MO: Mosby-Year Book, Inc., 1995), p 19.

[4] One suggested resource is the ABMP (Associated Bodywork and Massage Professionals) consumer education website: www.massagetherapy.com

Ways to Move Stuck Energy

- Acupuncture
- Acupressure, Shiatsu, Jin Shin Do
- Aromatherapy
- Cathartic Work
- Chanting
- Conscious Breath Work
- Cranio-sacral Therapy
- Creative Activities
- Dancing
- Detoxifying
- DNA Healing (energetic)
- Emotional Freedom Technique
- Essential Oils
- Exercise
- Feldenkrais
- Flower Essences
- Intuitive Healing
- Kinesiology
- Laughing
- Light Therapy
- Making Love
- Massage
- Meditation
- Myofascial Release
- Neuromuscular Therapy
- Playing a Musical Instrument
- Polarity Therapy
- Qi Gong
- Reflexology
- Reiki and Other Energy Work
- Rolfing
- Running the Kundalini
- Shamanic Healing
- Singing
- Sound Therapy
- Swimming
- Tai Chi
- Therapeutic Touch
- Toning
- Touch for Health
- Tui-na
- Walking
- Yoga
- Zero Balancing

Stuck energy will eventually manifest itself as a physical, mental, or emotional problem, or some combination of these. Using the above modalities to move the stuck energy can greatly relieve the symptoms. If the symptoms persist or keep returning each time the energy is moved, it probably means that the cause of the stuck energy has not been addressed.

Our body, emotions, and thoughts are tuned in to the soul, and are ways that our souls speak to us. If we pay attention to the sensations, discomfort, and disease in our bodies, we can locate the places where energy is stuck. Our emotions and thoughts can help us discern the cause of the stuck energy, which can then be healed with forgiveness.

The following exercise is designed to help you become aware of and heal the underlying causes of your stuck energy.

Exercise – Healing the Causes of Stuck Energy

1. *Ground yourself to the earth and your Higher Self. Ask your Higher Self and soul to guide you.*
2. *Focus in on your body. What sensations are you feeling? Is there a particular place of discomfort, or a mysterious sensation or sudden twinge somewhere?*
3. *As you focus on this area of your body, ask your Higher Self to reveal to you what is causing the energy to be stuck there. What thoughts are you thinking? What emotions are you feeling? What beliefs that no longer serve you come to your awareness? Let your Higher Self guide you through this process. You may get a vision, a word, a feeling, or a knowing related to what is causing the stuck energy.*
4. *Now ask your Higher Self to infuse you with the vibration of forgiveness to heal whatever has caused the energy to become stuck and to replace it with energy, thoughts, beliefs, etc. that are in alignment with your truth. Feel forgiveness healing this area of your body and aura, and healing all experiences related to the issue that has surfaced.*

When we move our stuck energy, we move ourselves out of the ruts that have caused us to feel stuck in our lives. As previously mentioned, every time an area of stuck energy is moved, the vibration of the body increases, allowing more of the soul to be present in the body. This makes a remarkable difference in our lives. For it is through the soul that we find the love, connectedness, wisdom, fulfillment, abundance, and sense of unity that we know is there, but has seemingly been just beyond our reach.

Moving stuck energy creates the space for another very important change to occur. It allows us to mend our lives by balancing and integrating our light and dark sides. This takes us out of polarity and helps us to see and live life from a whole new perspective. This is the perspective of the soul. It is balanced, expansive, and aware. It supports the highest good and unity of all. This perspective comes forth when we open the sixth portal to the soul. It is the portal through which we create the life of our dreams.

Balancing our energy
opens the sixth portal
to the soul.

Through this portal
we can see life from
the soul's perspective
and envision the life of
our dreams.

welcome to

The Sixth Portal

to your soul…

The Sixth Portal

Name	Sixth or Third Eye Chakra
Location	Center of the forehead
Traditional Color	Indigo blue
Functions	• Sees life from the soul's perspective • Integrates information from all the chakras into a clear vision, picture, or idea
Balanced Tendencies	Expanded awareness; unlimited potential; discernment; imagination; flexibility of thought; positive and balanced outlook on life that transcends judgment and polarity; balanced integration of right and left hemispheres of the brain and masculine and feminine sides
Unbalanced Tendencies	Short-sighted; closed-minded; narrow in perspective; overly intellectual; stuck in duality (seeing things as opposites); rigid; one-sided; impulsive; flighty; unrealistic; inability to focus
Physical Problems	Brain tumors; strokes; blindness; deafness; seizures; learning disabilities
Mental and Emotional Issues	Eccentric; confused; irrational; delusional; gender related issues and problems; unbalanced right and left brain activities
Restoring Validations	I look beyond outside appearances. I remain flexible in my perceptions and beliefs. I dissolve the illusions that no longer serve me. I integrate and balance that which appears to be opposite into wholeness and unity.

PORTAL #6

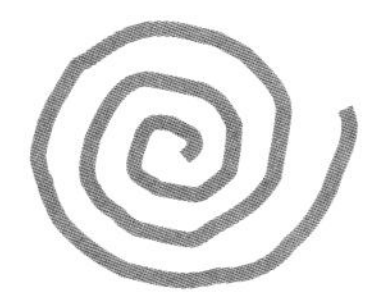

Create the Life of Your Dreams by Balancing Your Energy

What does the life of your dreams look like? Do you dream of a life filled with loving relationships—a life in which those around you care for you and fully encourage you to be who you are? Do you dream of a life of abundance—a life in which you have everything you need to live comfortably, without working so hard? Do you dream of a life in which you are totally fulfilled—a life in which you can do all the things you love to do, plus have free time just to "be"?

Most of us have spent time daydreaming about how we wish life could be. Some have even written down a vision for their lives. But for the majority of people, the reality of their present life falls far short of the life of their dreams.

I wrote down a vision for my life years ago. I dreamt of a life in which I felt good about myself, inside and out. I envisioned my home to be a haven—a place filled with peace, joy, and unconditional love. I wrote of supportive relationships in which my mate, my children, my friends, and I could flourish and totally be ourselves. I dreamt of a life in which I would wake up each morning greeting the new day with enthusiasm. I envisioned doing work that came from the soul—work that brought me fulfillment and made a contribution to the world. I wrote of a life where personal growth, fun, and laughter were paramount. I dreamt of a life in which the things I did each day were determined by guidance, intuition, passion, and joy.

That vision has become my reality. I love my life. It is the life of my dreams. How did I do it? By balancing my energy. Balancing our energy is one of the most important things we can do to create a better life. It synchronizes our bodies with our souls. It heals the wounds and self-sabotaging behaviors. It opens the sixth portal to the soul so that we can see life from the soul's perspective and envision the life of our dreams. It helps the chakras to work together to draw to us what is needed to bring that vision into reality. In this chapter, you will learn why balance is so important; how to determine where more balance is needed; and how to balance your energy to create the life of your dreams.

Why Balance?

Why is balance so important? How can balancing our energy help create the life of our dreams? Let's begin the understanding of the importance of balance by bringing to mind those times when it was needed.

Recall a time in your life when you struggled to gain your balance. Maybe it was when you were just learning how to ride a bicycle. Someone had to run along beside you to keep you from falling over. Or maybe it was the first time you rode in a boat. You ended up lurching back and forth until you found your "sea legs". Or maybe it was the first time you donned a pair of ice skates. Remember how they kept slipping out from under you?

Take yourself back in time to that moment of imbalance. Can you feel the lack of confidence, and the feelings of insecurity and unsteadiness that prevailed? Do you remember how afraid you were of getting hurt and the helpless reliance you had on others to assist you?

Unbalanced energy is much like that. When our energy is unbalanced, we feel unsure of ourselves—unsteady, scattered, lacking, and in need of assistance. Our fears take over. Life is lived from a mindset of alleviating fear rather than pursuing our passions.

> When our energy is unbalanced, we feel unsure of ourselves—unsteady, scattered, lacking, and in need of assistance.

When unbalanced, some people become afraid of not being good enough. In an attempt to eliminate this fear and prove their self-worth, they do things that do not give them joy. They work at jobs that provide little satisfaction. They do things out of obligation or because it is expected. When out of balance, some people become afraid of being hurt; so they go on the offensive, attacking others before they can be attacked. Or they put up defenses that keep them from loving unconditionally and end up hurting those who are closest to them.

When unbalanced, some people worry about not having what they need to survive. This leads to greed and hoarding, with some having more than they could ever use while others starve to death. Unbalanced energy puts our lives in distress. It gives us the feeling that we are constantly falling and failing, similar to what we felt each time that we tumbled off our bicycles.

Balanced energy is much different. Recall how good it felt when you finally found your balance: the exhilaration of riding your two-wheeler without help; the fun of feeling the waves beneath your feet as you stood up in the boat; and the pride of skating around the ice rink without falling down. Do you remember the sense of confidence, accomplishment, independence, and freedom you felt? Do you remember how satisfying that was?

Balanced energy is like that. When our energy is balanced, we feel good. We feel confident, expanded, solid, steady, free, independent, and whole. Our outlook on life changes when we are balanced. We are no longer driven by our fears. We are free to pursue our passions. We are confident that we have what it takes to live an abundant, loving, and joy-filled life. We know there will always be enough to live comfortably. We see others and ourselves as loving and lovable. We understand that we are part of the whole, where supporting the highest good of all is the best support we can give to ourselves. Balanced energy promotes peace, harmony, serenity, abundant living, and personal fulfillment.

Balanced energy promotes peace, harmony, serenity, abundant living, and personal fulfillment.

When our energy is balanced, we see and live life from a whole new perspective. This perspective allows us to see and create the life of our dreams. We gain access to this perspective through the sixth portal to the soul.

The Role of the Sixth Portal to the Soul

Also known as the third eye, the sixth chakra is our visionary center. It is located at the center of the forehead. The third eye is the portal through which we see our lives from the soul's perspective. But we will not see life from this perspective unless we are balanced. We will instead see it from a skewed and limited perspective, as if we were tipped to one side.

Being tipped to one side causes us to be shortsighted and narrow-focused. It causes us to lose sight of the big picture. It may cause us to focus exclusively on the material side of life, not seeing the spiritual side of it—or vice versa. It may cause us to pursue goals that do not bring fulfillment. There are many books written on how to achieve one's goals and how to manifest one's desires. But unless these desires come directly from the soul, they will not bring true happiness. They will not support the life of one's dreams.

Unless our desires come directly from the soul, they will not bring true happiness.

How many times have you seen people suffer through the stress of climbing the corporate ladder and then encounter a life of emptiness, loneliness, and even boredom at the top? How often do you see people rushing after things that they think will bring them joy, only to become disappointed when they finally get them? How frequently have you yourself experienced the fleeting happiness of a goal you've attained?

The shortsighted desires and goals of the mind and ego may bring short-term enjoyment; but they are never enough. They cause us to want more, becoming dissatisfied with what we have. The ego acts like a child at Christmas, who tears open one package after another, barely paying attention to the gift within. And then, after the last package is unwrapped, he or she looks around for more. How does one stop this meaningless and hollow quest for happiness? We do it by opening our third eye—the sixth portal to our soul.

The more we open the third eye, the more expanded our vision becomes. This is important, because we create through our thoughts. A person who thinks big thoughts is better able to create big things. A person whose thoughts are limited by a narrow vision creates a limited life. The limitations we place upon ourselves begin to disappear as we balance our energy and open the third eye.

The third eye is our personal window to the world of the soul. Through this window the soul gives us a picture that is more encompassing, accurate, expansive, and balanced than any picture created by the mind through the physical eyes. It goes beyond the limitations and boundaries of physicality, time, and space. My own soul illustrated for me how little we see with the physical eyes versus the third eye.

Just prior to starting work on this chapter, I was printing out the previous chapter. The printer did something that it had never done before. Rather than printing a full page of type, it printed five to seven solid black lines on each page. There was empty space between each line equivalent to the size of a paragraph. After looking at it closely, I realized that each paragraph had been printed on only one line of type. All the words of the paragraph were mashed together into one black line, followed by empty space where the rest of the paragraph would have been.

I chuckled and asked my soul what it was trying to show me. It said that we miss a whole lot when we don't see life from the soul's perspective. It appears to be black and white because everything ends up on one straight line. The third eye is able to decode this mess and show us the multifaceted, multidimensional, and multidirectional nuances of life. What we think of as the void, or the space between the lines, is the "essential unseen". It is the stuff of which life is really made.

Rebooting the computer took care of the printing problem. Opening the third eye, and seeing things from the soul's perspective, requires a rebooting of the mind. Research has indicated that we use only about ten percent of the mind's capabilities. Ninety percent goes unused. Imagine the detail of a picture taken using a six megapixel (six million pixels) digital camera and then using only a few thousand of those pixels to print it out. We do something similar to that when we depend on our physical

Opening the third eye, and seeing things from the soul's perspective, requires a rebooting of the mind.

eyes to capture our perceptions of the world. We miss most of what is there. We miss much of the essential unseen. Once the mind is rebooted (reconfigured), the soul is able to download a much more detailed picture to it through the third eye. You will learn how to do that further along in this chapter. Through the third eye, we are able to see well below the surface into other time/space continuums and dimensions.

One afternoon I was massaging my partner's back, as I had done numerous times. I was surprised to see a very long scar along his spine that I had never noticed before. When I asked him about it, he told me to trace it with my finger. The jagged line I traced matched up exactly with the injury he had received from a fall down the inside of a silo 25 years earlier. I was seeing "back in time". The scar was no longer visible to the physical eyes, but could be seen through the third eye.

When the third eye is closed, we perceive a world of limitation. We see a finite world of impossibilities, laced with lack and despair. When the third eye is open, we perceive a world of unlimited possibilities. We see a world of abundance and promise, the only boundary of which is the outer limit of our imagination.

When the third eye is open, we perceive a world of unlimited possibilities.

Why is there such a difference? The third eye sees far beyond what can be perceived by the physical eyes. It gathers information from many sources. These include such things as intuition and knowing, emotions and feelings, and psychic inputs such as clairvoyance, clairaudience, and clairsentience. It sees the unseen and sifts through the illusions that appear to be "real".

The third eye then integrates all of this information and presents the mind with a conclusion, picture, or vision of what is happening. This is a much broader and more balanced picture than what the brain alone can provide. The third eye and the mind are meant to work together. But because for most of us the third eye has been "closed", we are missing much of the information and insight that comes from the soul. We have come to believe that "what we see (with the physical eyes) is what we get". This is very misleading.

When we depend on our physical eyes to show us what we think is "real" and when we depend on our minds and egos to direct us based on what we think we see and know, we get ourselves into trouble. We perceive life from a skewed, linear, limited, and oftentimes negative, perspective. This creates fear. It leads us to believe that we are victims of inevitable suffering. It prevents us from creating the life of our dreams. We create a life based on illusion and then wonder why it feels so empty.

When we rely on the third eye to show us what *is* real, and when we depend on the Higher Self to guide us based upon what it *knows* to be true, then we have the information we need to create the life of our dreams. We create a vision for life that is in alignment with the soul's essence and purpose—a life that brings us joy, satisfaction, and fulfillment. A life of unlimited possibilities becomes possible when we open the third eye.

When we rely on the third eye to show us what *is* real, and when we depend on the Higher Self to guide us based upon what it *knows* to be true, then we have the information we need to create the life of our dreams.

It is the job of the sixth chakra to help us perceive things in balance, and in alignment, with the soul's perspective. That is why balancing our energy is so important to the opening and functioning of the third eye.

Are You Balanced?

How do we know whether we are balanced? We can take a look at our lives. They are a reflection of our inner condition. Ask yourself the following questions.

Is there peace in your home? Is your environment harmonious outside the home (work, school, volunteer activities)? Do you feel you have everything you need to live? Do you love what you do each day? Do you like who you are? Are your relationships supportive and loving? Do you love your life?

If you can answer *yes* to all these questions, then you are balanced. Your life is probably the life of your dreams. If you answered *no* to any of the questions above, what seems to be the problem? Are you frustrated with your life? Is there strife in your home? Is your life outside the home chaotic or upsetting? Are you worried and anxious? Is there something about yourself that disturbs you? Do the things you do each day give you little joy? Are there problems in your relationships? Are you afraid of not having what you need to live? Do you wish your life were different? If you answered *yes* to any of these questions, then balance will help you to create the life of your dreams.

Signs of Internal Imbalance

We have become quite good at recognizing when certain parts of our lives are out of balance. For example, too many sweets make us feel ill. Burning the candle at both ends makes us feel tired. Putting in 60-70 hour workweeks causes us to feel overworked. Constantly being with other people can make us feel "peopled-out".

When we are out of balance in these areas of our lives, we usually know why. We begin to tell ourselves, "I need to eat better"; "I need a vacation"; or "I need some alone time". We have become proficient at knowing when things like these are out of balance—even if we don't always do what it takes to bring them back into balance!

There seems to be greater difficulty in knowing when the inner self is unbalanced. It may not be a familiar concept. But we have all felt it. When we are out of balance internally, we don't feel right. We feel edgy, cranky, confused, fearful, wound up, or "off". But unlike some of the more obvious areas of our lives, most of us don't always recognize the problem as being one of imbalance. Even fewer know what to do about it. So let us begin by learning the symptoms, and then we will focus on the solutions.

We have several indicators of whether or not we are in balance internally. These include our:

- **Thoughts**
- **Emotions**
- **Behaviors**
- **Physical Sensations**

Thoughts

If our thoughts are running rampant, disjointed, disruptive, negative, divisive, or judgmental, it is a sign that something is out of balance. If, on the other hand, our thoughts are calm, peaceful, focused, unifying, and uplifting, it is a sign that we are in balance.

Thoughts about other people can tell us a great deal about our internal state of affairs. Other people tend to bring our areas of imbalance to the surface. We will use Celeste as an example. Celeste met an interesting man at the singles gathering last week. Celeste thought they hit it off. She gave him her phone number, but he has not called her for a date.

> Thoughts about other people can tell us a great deal about our internal state of affairs.

Celeste's thoughts about this situation can tell her many things about herself. Celeste might start to concoct all kinds of reasons why the young man didn't call. She might judge herself to be homely, stupid, or boring. These thoughts show Celeste how she really feels about herself. She might decide that this man is "just like all the other men", out for a good time, but not interested in commitment. These thoughts indicate her prejudices about the male gender. Negative and judgmental thoughts toward self or others can show us where we are in need of balancing.

If, on the other hand, Celeste can simply acknowledge that the man didn't call and let it go at that without deriding herself or the man for it, it is a sign that Celeste has some balance in this area.

Monitoring our thoughts can help us to find our areas of imbalance. Many of our negative thoughts are just below the surface. They destroy our peace of mind even when we aren't consciously thinking of them. Pretending that others can read our thoughts helps to bring these destructive thoughts to the surface to be healed. It makes us more conscious of them.

Pretending that others can read our thoughts helps to bring destructive thoughts to the surface to be healed.

Emotions

Our emotions are another indicator of whether or not we are in balance. If our thoughts haven't gotten our attention, perhaps our emotions will. Emotions such as depression, hatred, regret, revenge, anxiety, fear, guilt, and shame are indicators that something is out of balance. The emotions of joy, peace, compassion, acceptance, and unconditional love are indicators of being in balance. (Notice how many more descriptors we have for unbalanced energy than we do for balanced energy. It is a good indication of how off-balance we have been!)

Celeste might start to feel depressed or anxious over the fact that the young man didn't call—a further sign to her that something is out of balance. Or, she might feel acceptance and peace, with no attachment to the outcome of that meeting—a sign of balance. Monitoring our emotions can tell us a lot about our internal states of being.

Behaviors

Our behaviors are a third indicator of whether or not we are in balance. When we don't pay attention to our unbalanced thoughts or emotions, we may start acting them out. Or we may unconsciously sabotage ourselves. For example, Celeste might start "bad-mouthing" the man that never called her. Or she may decide not to give out her phone number anymore. If we find ourselves in a reactionary mode, lashing out at others, defensive, hurtful, or unkind, it is a sign that something within is unbalanced.

If our energy is balanced, our actions will show that too. In that case, Celeste could pick up the phone and make the first call, or she might dismiss the matter altogether. If we find ourselves to be in harmony with all that is around us, exhibiting behaviors that foster the highest good of all, it is a sign that we are in balance.

> If we find ourselves to be in harmony with all that is around us, exhibiting behaviors that foster the highest good of all, it is a sign that we are in balance.

Physical Sensations

Our physical sensations are a fourth indicator of whether or not we are in balance. Celeste's strong emotional upset over the situation could actually cause her to get sick or to feel pain somewhere in her body. Physical maladies oftentimes show up when there are unresolved issues related to areas of imbalance.

Have you ever "made yourself sick" with worry or grief? Have you ever gotten headaches, a "nervous stomach", an ulcer, or high blood pressure, from anxiety or stress? Do you sometimes feel the weight of the world sitting upon your shoulders?

The body is an excellent barometer of our state of being. Our physical health ultimately is related to the movement and balance of our energy. So it really is not very difficult to determine whether we are in balance. We can know it by our thoughts, emotions, behaviors, and physical symptoms. We just need to be willing to play the role of observer, rather than the role of victim.

The body is an excellent barometer of our state of being.

How to Regain Our Balance

So what do we do about it? When we observe that we have an area, which is out of balance, how do we bring it back into balance? There are three important things we can do. Each of them also helps to further open the sixth portal to the soul. They are:

1. **Balance our light and dark energies**
2. **Balance our masculine and feminine sides**
3. **Balance our chakras**

We will address these one by one. None of them are one-time events. They are processes. You will be given techniques for each to help you through the process. Each time you balance something, you will feel better about yourself and your life. The process will continue long after you finish this book. Your soul and Higher Self will bring things to your awareness, as you are ready to acknowledge, heal, and integrate them. So let go, allow the process to be what it is, and enjoy the ride!

1. Balance the Light and Dark Energies

One of the marvelous gifts of life on earth is the experience of "self". The "self" is a complex mixture of many kinds of energies. Some are light. Some are dark. Coming to an understanding of these energies is a lifelong pursuit. In every situation and encounter, we have the chance to discover something about our makeup—our gifts, attributes, traits, and energies. The earth is an exceptionally unique place where we have the opportunity to look at and experience our individual energies as if through a microscope. Energy moves slowly here, so we can get a very close look at it.

> One of the marvelous gifts of life on earth is the experience of "self".

Light and Dark Energies

Imagine energy to be similar to the components of vinaigrette dressing. When it is shaken (moved very fast), it becomes a homogeneous liquid. When it stands still, the oil and vinegar separate. Energy in the higher dimensions appears to be homogeneous because it is moving so fast. Here on earth, where the energy moves so slowly, the individual components can more easily be distinguished. Oil floats on top of vinegar because it is lighter in density. The energies we experience are also of differing densities. We call the heavier energies "dark" and the less dense energies "light". They are separated out so that we can experience their unique properties.

The dark energies are a necessary component of the experience of "self". They create the boundaries that differentiate one thing from another. They allow us to have individual bodies, individual souls, and a physical existence. In small amounts, the dark energies are critical to our physicality. Without the dark energies, all of physicality would vanish. We would not have a physical body, nor would we have our homes, chocolate cake, or a table at which to eat it. Fido would be a figment of our imagination. And life as we know it would "disappear". Everything would dissolve into one mass of energy. That is because it is the darker, denser energies that separate and contract energy.

Just as the dark energies separate us one from another, the lighter energies join us together. The light energies expand, connect, and unify. They help us feel connected to ourselves, others, and All That Is. It is the light energies that keep our energy moving and expanding. Without them, we would feel totally isolated and alone. They help us to live together, support one another, work together, and unify us for the common good of all.

Our individual energetic light and dark components are meant to be combined and integrated in balanced proportions. If they are dis-integrated and out of balance, they don't feel right. Nor do they work well. Too much light energy can prevent us from having an experience of "self". Too much dark energy can make us totally selfish. Too much of either one can prevent us from having a sustainable and pleasurable physical existence.

Too much light energy can prevent us from having an experience of "self". Too much dark energy can make us totally selfish.

It is the *balance* of energy that fashions the lives we have always dreamed of having. Let's return to the vinaigrette analogy to see why. When the lighter oil and the denser vinegar are in balanced proportions, we have a tasty dressing. When they are out of proportion, we get either a bitter or an oily taste on the tongue. A similar thing happens when the light and dark energies are out of proportion. If there is an excess of dark energy, life becomes bitter and hard to swallow. If there is an excess of light energy, physical life becomes slippery and difficult to sustain.

Imbalances create pain. Have you ever eaten or drank so much that you became sick to your stomach? Have you ever stayed in the sun so long that your skin blistered? Have you ever had so much rain that your basement flooded? We call these experiences painful or "bad". But it is not the food, sun, or rain that is bad. It is having too much of them that can be bad for us. Not having them at all would be really bad!

The same is true of anything that is out of balance. This includes what we call dark and light energies. Both energies are part of All That Is. Both are inherently good and necessary. It is the *imbalance* of dark and light energy that makes our lives so unpleasant.

> It is the *imbalance* of dark and light energy that makes our lives so unpleasant.

There has been an excess of the dark energies, at least throughout recorded history. Our emotional response to this excess of dark energy is recognized as fear, judgment, rage, revenge, guilt, depression, shame, greed, etc. We have labeled the excess of dark energies "bad" or "evil" because they have contributed to painful conditions: things like war, abuse, control, oppression, prejudice, and poverty. The dark energies themselves are not bad. But having such an excess of them has been a bitter pill to swallow.

> The intent in this physical plane is to experience the various individual energies that cause us to appear separate while at the same time experiencing the connection and unity of All That Is.

The intent in this physical plane is to experience the various individual energies that cause us to appear separate while at the same time experiencing the connection and unity of All That Is. This provides the optimum experience for us—one that is joyful, peaceful, loving and, at the same time, physical. But it only happens when the balance of the light and dark energies is finely tuned.

The imbalance of energy makes our personal lives difficult to endure. It also creates hardship and adversity in the world at large. We are in the process of bringing the energetic polarities of our world into balance and unity. What seems like a monumental task is already well underway. The polarities are coming to the surface to be looked at and experienced. That is why we have been seeing so much chaos in our lives, our governments, corporations, religious institutions, and world events. The old ways of doing things are dissolving. We are seeing the flaws of a world governed by duality. Now is the time to regroup and create a new paradigm. That new paradigm is balance.

As we each balance our inner selves, we automatically create a life that is balanced. Balance is not something that we get from the world. It is something that we give to it. Our lives are not dependent upon the state of the world. The state of the world is dependent upon the state of our lives. The world will become the balanced world of our dreams when we balance the energy within ourselves. *It is up to us to do it.* Only *we* can create the life and world of our dreams. Each of us has an important part to play in this. You will see how it is done shortly.

Balance is not something that we get from the world. It is something that we give to it.

Let's first take a moment to understand how the balancing of energy occurs so that you can flow with it as it happens.

Through a couple of examples, you will sense what to look for and expect throughout this amazing process.

Energy Families

Energies are balanced according to their energy family. The various aspects of an energy family are designed to work together to assist us in living a harmonious physical existence. When balanced, the energies within an energy family perform specific functions that contribute toward a common purpose. When out of balance, the energies appear to work against each other. We are in the process of joining back together the various facets of these energy families—energies that we have, until now, perceived to be opposites.

> When balanced, the energies within an energy family perform specific functions that contribute toward a common purpose.

Let us use, as an example, the energies of rage, anger, and forgiveness. It may surprise you to know that these energies are part of the same energy family. One purpose of this energy family is to create the simultaneous experience of *uniqueness in unity.* At the same time that we know and feel our individuality, we come to know, feel, and appreciate the oneness we have with all else. There is a divine harmony established that allows us to experience the separation of self and unity with all else at the same time.

Anger and forgiveness are not at odds with one another, as we have believed. They are meant to work together. It is helpful to keep in mind that it is the *imbalance* of energy that has caused us to experience the extreme polarities of an energy family, calling them opposites.

We will take a look at these energies individually in order to understand how they fit together. Let's start with rage. Rage is the energy that helps us to set our boundaries. It is a very dense energy, which can become violent when out of balance. It may cause us to lash out, distance ourselves from others, and even do harm mentally, emotionally, or physically. All this is an attempt to move our boundaries back to a place where we feel safe and to maintain our individuality. Rage is meant to be present and used in small amounts. A little bit of rage goes a long way. In small amounts, it does not at all look or feel like the ranting, raving, maniacal or brutal force that we have been exposed to in the past. When in balance, rage helps us to set boundaries that are honoring to ourselves without hurting others.

Anger, which is part of the same energy family, is less dense than rage. Its purpose is to show us when it is time to establish or reestablish a boundary. Our anger is a signal to us that something within us is not being honored. If we don't pay attention to our anger, or if we submerge it, we are likely to let people "walk all over us", losing our individuality. This may eventually come out as rage, during which time we try to reestablish our boundaries.

Our anger is a signal to us that something within us is not being honored.

Forgiveness is on the light end of this energy family. Forgiveness brings people, memories, experiences, and other energies back into wholeness or unity. I have previously referred to it as a "zipping" energy, because it zips other energies together into unity. Forgiveness is one of the energies that help us to draw together as One.

Without the boundary setting energies that we call anger and rage, we would become like a herd of sheep. There would be a tendency to zip back together into a soup of miscellaneous energy and lose our individuality. Without the unifying energy we call forgiveness, we would lose our sense of oneness and connection with all else. We would create impenetrable walls between us.

Until this energy family is balanced within, separation and unity seem paradoxical. When tipped toward the dark end of the energy family, we feel isolated and alone. When tipped the other way, we lose our sense of self. An imbalance in either direction causes us to perceive life from a narrow and skewed perspective. As these energies come into balance, we usually tip back and forth for a while, with the strong polarities coming forth before finally coming together into balance.

When balanced, the paradox disappears. The third eye opens a little more, and the soul is able to show us how we as individuals are One. We see that everything we do to or for another is done to or for ourselves. We live with much more caring, kindness, and integrity—for each other, the earth, and ourselves. Have you seen this happening in your life? It is beginning to happen in the world.

> As anger and forgiveness come into balance, the soul is able to show us how we as individuals are One.

The process of balancing and unifying this energy family has been evident in the polarity following the devastation and loss of life in the United States that occurred on September 11, 2001. There was an outburst of anger and rage on the one hand, and an outpouring of forgiveness and caring on the other.

Anger caused us to rethink our boundaries. There was a revival of nationalism and patriotism, a tightening of our borders, increased security, and beefed up defenses. Rage caused us to lash out at others, declaring war on terrorism, attacking other countries, and destroying lives and property.

At the other end of the energy spectrum, we saw an increase in the feeling of unity among the people of the world as prayers were offered and money, food, supplies, good wishes, and letters of support were sent to those affected by the tragedy here and abroad. The energy of forgiveness came through loud and clear, helping to balance the anger and the rage.

People became polarized about the war. There was a strong outcry for war and an equally strong protest for peace. Not only were people within our country divided on the issue, but also countries across the world took sides. This was all part of the preliminary balancing process. The pendulum was swinging back and forth between the light and dark to expose the individual components of this energy family. It was a very good, albeit painful, way to take a close look at the energies of this family prior to their integration. The pendulum seems to swing most erratically just prior to the final balancing.

Another example of an energy family that is coming into unity is that of fear, compassion, and love. One purpose of this energy family is to foster attraction based on common resonance. When this energy family is in balance, it helps people, who resonate to a common soul vibration and purpose, to be brought together. They are attracted to that which resonates with their souls, and not attracted to that which does not resonate. When this energy family is out of balance, it either keeps people separate or causes people who do not resonate at the soul level to come together. Let's take a look at the energies of this family to see why.

> **When the energy family of fear, compassion, and love is in balance, it helps people, who resonate to a common soul vibration and purpose, to be brought together.**

Fear is the energy of protection. It helps to keep us safe. The vibration of fear "tips us off" to things that can harm us or that do not resonate with us. Fear is such a dense energy, however, that, when it is unbalanced, it can veil the true energy of our souls. Like attracts like, so people then tend to be drawn together and polarized according to their fears. Unbalanced fear is one of the major forces behind such things as prejudice, racism, caste systems, and religious fanaticism.

Fear condenses our energy. Fear is the energy of withdrawal, of pulling back, or shrinking back. Unbalanced fear forms a kind of shell around us. Strong fears keep us from pursuing our hopes and our dreams. They prevent us from using our power, gifts, and abilities. Fear keeps us from fully being and expressing who we are. Fear is similar in density to rage. A little bit of fear goes a long way.

Fear keeps us from fully being and expressing who we are.

Love and compassion represent the lighter side of the energy family. Compassion is expansive. It fosters equality. It underlies the principle that all people are created equal and have an equal right to their earthly experiences. Compassion helps us to accept unconditionally all that we are.

Love is our connection with each other, the Universe, and ourselves. Pure love eliminates boundaries. We are one because of love. Love causes us to be freely drawn together. Fear adds an element of selectivity to that attraction, based upon resonance. When love and fear are in balance, we draw to us the people and circumstances that support the divine plan for our lives.

The following analogy may help to add meaning to the fear-compassion-love energy family. Imagine a drop of water on waxed paper or a newly waxed car; it beads up. That is because the waxy surface increases the surface tension of the water. Fear is comparable to the wax. The more fear introduced into a situation, the more beaded up, or withdrawn, the energy of the individual or group becomes. Fear causes people to shun parts of themselves and to separate themselves from others.

Love causes energies to spread out. It acts much like a surfactant that lowers the surface tension of water, enabling it to spread out over a surface. Love can dissolve fear. The surfactants in soap help the water to become "wetter"—to freely interact and blend with, or dissolve, dirt, grease, and stains. When love is added to other energies, it increases their ability to interact with one another.

Compassion puts everything on an equal plane. Compassion perceives both states of water to be perfectly acceptable and valid. It makes no judgment regarding the goodness or badness of water that is beaded up versus water that is flowing. It makes no judgment between beads of water, beads of oil, or beads of mercury. Compassion understands that each serves a purpose.

When the energy family of love, compassion, and fear are in balance, we feel safe and accepted. We draw people with whom we can live and work in harmony to us—people who share a common purpose and passion. We also allow the experience, of those with whom we do not resonate, to be what it is without judgment. As this energy family comes into balance internally, the third eye opens a little more. The soul is able to give us a new perspective on how we can live and work together in collaboration, rather than in competition. People move in and out of our lives to support our soul purpose. Our relationships improve dramatically.

> As the third eye opens, the soul is able to give us a new perspective on how we can live and work together.

What are some of the other energy families that are being balanced and integrated? A partial list is given below. These are not absolutes. They are just examples. You may have other ways of organizing the various energies according to your understanding and experience of them.

Energy Families

- Abundance & Lack
- Acceptance & Resistance
- Collaboration & Competition
- Cooperation & Defiance
- Expression & Silence
- Flexibility & Rigidity
- Freedom & Constraint
- Harmony & Discord
- Honesty & Deceit
- Honor & Humiliation
- Hope & Despair
- Integrity & Corruption
- Justice & Unfairness
- Kindness & Cruelty
- Peace & Turmoil
- Perseverance & Irresolution
- Power & Control
- Sovereignty & Codependency
- Strength & Weakness
- Structure & Chaos
- Trust & Distrust
- Truth & Fantasy
- Understanding & Confusion

Your Energy Families

Each of us focuses on balancing some energy families more than others. The ones that we individually concentrate on have to do with the discovery of self. They are the "lessons" we are to experience. These lessons are based on our soul essences. We experience fully certain aspects of our soul, both in the "positive" and in the "negative".

Each of us focuses on balancing some energy families more than others.

One of my energy families contains the energies of freedom and constraint. I have explored in depth many of the energies in the freedom-constraint family. I have experienced attachment, detachment, dependence, codependence, independence, control, free will, choice, and lack of choice, to name a few. What may have appeared to me in the past to be a tug and pull between freedom and constraint was really all part of the same lesson or experience. My soul wanted to know and experience all that it could about this part of its essence prior to balancing and integrating it.

Which energy families have been most evident in your life? Ask yourself the following questions to help you determine which energy families you may need to balance.

1. What traits have caused you to feel like Dr. Jeckyll and Mr. Hyde?
2. Have there been certain polarities in your personality that have surfaced again and again?
3. Have you had a propensity for flipping back and forth between two "opposite" kinds of behavior?
4. What do you appreciate about yourself?
5. What do you wish you could change about yourself?
6. How have you unconsciously sabotaged yourself?

7. What qualities do you admire or criticize in other people?

The answers to these questions are clues pointing to the soul essences and energy families that you are working on balancing and integrating.

Balancing Your Energy Families

How do we balance our energy families—those essences of our souls that have seemingly worked against each other? A common tendency is to try to control each dark side. We try to submerge it or make it smaller. We order it into its own little corner like a misbehaving child having a "time out". We judge it, hate it, beat up on it, and ignore it, hoping that it will come under our control or just go away. We hide our fears, ignore our sadness, set aside our resistance, and stuff our anger. We have seen that this doesn't work. These areas of darkness come back to sabotage us at the most undesirable and unsuspecting times.

Regardless of whether we stuff our dark sides consciously or unconsciously, what we end up with is a tight ball of stuck dark energy through which it becomes very difficult for other energies to penetrate. Many times we experience this as tightness in our bodies, similar to Kathy's golf ball sized knot that was addressed in the last chapter.

Judging ourselves increases the strength and tenacity of the darkness. What we resist persists. What we focus on becomes stronger. When we judge something, we are resisting it and focusing in on it at the same time. We put energy into it, making it stronger than ever.

When we judge something, we put energy into it, making it stronger than ever.

To illustrate this concept, I will relate an incident I had when in a group of people. One of the ladies took out a very strong essential oil, and put some on herself. The smell permeated the room. I could not get away from it. To her, this was a healing balm. To me, it was annoying. It began to give me a headache. I felt as if it were right in my face, even though she was across the room.

I started to think of ways that I could approach her to ask her politely to leave her essential oils at home next time. The more I thought about it, the worse was my reaction to the scent. I finally realized that I was in strong judgment of the situation. I decided to let go of my resistance and accept it. As soon as I made that decision, the odor became less obvious to me. It was no longer an annoyance. My judgment and resistance had contracted my energy and caused me to perceive the situation to be worse than it was. I was adding dark energy to it. Perhaps you have had a similar experience, where someone's body odor or perfume was offensive to you. The more you focused on it, the worse it became.

This is what happens when we judge our dark sides. We make the "problem" bigger, thus increasing its strength, and magnifying its hold on us. If I say or do something unkind to another and then keep vilifying myself for having done this, the memory stays with me. It won't go away. It keeps eating away at me. If, however, I can accept and forgive myself for what I have done, learn from it, and decide to choose differently next time, the gnawing feeling of guilt goes away. I can get on with my life.

The way to address our dark sides is not to get rid of them. The way to balance our dark sides, and their corresponding energy families, is to add more light to them. This is exactly the opposite of what we are inclined to do. It does not help to hate our hatred, resist our resistance, or fear our fear. It does not help to stuff them into a corner or tell them to

The way to address our dark sides is not to get rid of them.

go away. It does help us to face them, accept them, and balance them with lighter energies.

It takes a great deal of light energy to balance out a small amount of the denser dark energy. We are receiving tremendous amounts of light energy at this time to do just that—energies like unconditional love, hope, compassion, freedom, and forgiveness.

How do we bring in these light energies to balance our energy families? We do it the same way that we have been bringing in the vibration of forgiveness throughout the exercises in this book. We bring them in via our grounding cords to the earth and our Higher Selves. You will be given an exercise to walk you through this. But first, let me tell you about the vibrations that you will be using to balance your energy families.

The first vibration used is hope. Hope activates. It gets things moving. Hope helps whole cities to rebuild after a devastating tornado or flood. When balancing our energy, we use hope to begin to move the stuck areas of tightly knotted dark energies (like fear, judgment, control, etc.)

Hope, once it has begun to move and rearrange the energy, makes the way for compassion. Compassion's job is to expand other energies. It expands our awareness and gets us "outside ourselves". Energetically, compassion loosens the areas of agglomerated dark energy much like one would loosen the knots in a tangled fishing line or a fine chain necklace. More space is made within the tight bundles of energy.

This space is necessary in order that other light energies can come in and balance out the dark energies that are already present. The Higher Self directs which light energies are to come in to balance the dark energies. It might call upon the vibration of

The Higher Self directs which light energies are to come in to balance the dark energies.

flexibility to balance an area of rigidity in the neck or joints. It might bring up the vibration of abundance to heal the fear of not having enough, lodged in the lower back or sacrum.

When the lighter vibrations are introduced, both the light and dark energies may be felt simultaneously—for example, flexibility and rigidity, or abundance and lack. It may feel as if one is swinging back and forth on a pendulum, feeling the dark, and then feeling the light—back and forth—until balance and integration occur. This is the same sort of thing that occurred with the energies of rage and forgiveness following the devastation of 9-11.

Love, added to all the energies present, helps them freely interact with one another. Love dissolves the shells surrounding the energies so that what was separated, encapsulated, and polarized can merge together. As we bring our energies into balance, it is important to surround them in love. Love allows whatever we are balancing to be freely drawn together and integrated.

Love allows whatever we are balancing to be freely drawn together and integrated.

The final energy is forgiveness. Forgiveness zips the light and dark energies back together into wholeness. Voila! The balancing is complete. We are zipping together the various energies that we have experienced, at a very rapid rate. We see the polarities of these energies most strongly just prior to their integration. Sometimes they come to our awareness through the current events of the world. Other times we see them in a more personal, internal way.

Balancing Energy in the Body

It was pointed out previously that our thoughts, emotions, behaviors, and physical pain could be indicators of unbalanced energy. I have used the energies described above to relax and balance painful trigger points in my body. This works well during massage.

As the massage therapist applied pressure to several trigger points on my back, I set the intention to bring in the energies of hope, compassion, love, and forgiveness. I also asked my Higher Self to fill me with whatever other energies were needed to balance out what was already there.

I had a knot of resistance in my mid-back. It began to vibrate and move when hope was introduced. It expanded and became less dense when compassion was brought in. My Higher Self then included the energy of acceptance to balance it. I felt the separate energies of resistance, then acceptance, back and forth.

My Higher Self began to show me what had caused the resistance, and how it was working against me. I was shown that I had had an experience of betrayal a long, long time ago. I had depended on someone to provide something for me, and was let down.

The resistance from that situation was keeping me from fully accepting nurturance from the Universe through others. (I had a penchant for wanting to do things myself, and it was not allowing abundance to flow in my life). I acknowledged this behavior, and let it go, by resolving the karma behind it. The energies of resistance and acceptance were then balanced and integrated through forgiveness. These are part of the same energy family. I was helping to balance it.

My neck was another area of my body that held stuck, unbalanced energy. As tight spots on my neck received pressure by the therapist, I "saw" in my mind, two stiff rods going up either side of my cervical spine. This was the energy of rigidity.

Rigidity helps us to stay focused on a task until we complete it. The mind pulls in a lot of rigid energy when trying to find a solution to a problem. Decisions that require a broad focus must come from the soul, not the mind.

Many people experience tightness in their necks when they try to resolve problems through logic rather than through the soul's guidance. This is one of many things that can cause muscle spasms in the neck and head, often leading to headaches.

My Higher Self brought in the vibration of flexibility to balance the rigidity. I could feel both until they were integrated by forgiveness. When we balance such energies within ourselves, we also help to balance them in the world.

Our bodies hold a great deal of information, if we just take the time to listen to them. Where there are chronic problems, such as tight, tense muscles, there are usually stored issues to be addressed. Many of these are old and deep. Some are multifaceted and complex. Each time that energy is moved and balanced, and issues are healed, the body feels some relief from the symptoms. But it may take multiple sessions over a period of time before that area of the body is completely symptom free.

Where there are chronic problems, such as tight, tense muscles, there are usually stored issues to be addressed.

You are invited to try balancing some energy for yourself, using the exercise on the following page to guide you. Locate an area of your body where you have a trigger point or an area of pain. Or consider parts of your personality that have tended to work against each other. You can do this with or without another's assistance. You may want to try it both ways to see which is more effective for you. I have found, personally, that for most issues, I can integrate my energy by myself. But for my deepest issues, it is helpful to have the energy of another assist me.

As with everything else, there may be layers to gradually work through. So be patient with yourself, and allow your Higher Self to guide you through the multi-layered process of your healing. There may be weeks or months in between the peeling of the layers, and you may wonder why you have to deal with the "same thing" again and again. In actuality, the peeling process takes you deeper and deeper into the core of the issue each time it is addressed. Our strongest soul essences seem to require the most attention.

Exercise – Balancing Your Energy

1. *Locate a place in your body where you think the energy is stuck and unbalanced. It may be a trigger point, a sore or injured area, a tight muscle, or a place of disease.*

   - or -

   Select internal traits that appear to be polarized. The answers to the questions you answered on page 197, about energies you may need to balance, may be helpful.

2. *If you located an area of physical discomfort, place your hand on that area, or apply pressure to it, but not to the point of being uncomfortable.*

3. *Ground yourself to the earth and your Higher Self. Intend that you be infused with the vibration of hope. Allow hope to begin to move and rearrange the energies for a few moments.*

4. *Next bring in the vibration of compassion. Allow compassion to expand the energies that have been tied up in a ball. As they unwind and expand, pay attention to what you feel. Allow your conscious awareness to sink into the area of expanded energy.*

5. *Ask your Higher Self to reveal to you anything that is important to know regarding the energy that is stuck and unbalanced. Record your findings. What are the energies that are unbalanced? What thoughts, beliefs, and behaviors are contributing to the polarization of these energies and your personality?*
6. *Ask your Higher Self if there is unresolved karma involved. If so, ask it to bring to your awareness whatever is important for you to know about it. Then release the karma.*
7. *Ask your Higher Self to bring in whatever vibrations are needed to balance the energies. Your feelings may oscillate back and forth between the light side and the dark side of the energies. What are they? Record them.*
8. *Send love to the affected area of your body and to any of the associated energies, thoughts, beliefs, issues, or behaviors that your Higher Self showed you to be part of it.*
9. *Bring in the vibration of forgiveness. Allow forgiveness to balance and integrate the energies that have come forth, zipping them together.*
10. *Ask your Higher Self to replace the old negative thought forms and behaviors with new thoughts, beliefs, and behaviors that resonate with and support the balanced energy. Write down any that come to mind.*
11. *Feel the release, the opening, the sense of wholeness, and the peace.*

You may use this exercise to balance your shadow side, polarized parts of your personality, or any energy that is stuck. Play with it. You may find all kinds of fears, regrets, emotions, behaviors, thoughts, and judgments surfacing to be healed.

You may ask your Higher Self to take charge of the process, bringing in the various energies at the appropriate times. That way you can free up your mind to focus your awareness on what you are feeling, learning, and experiencing.

We learn a great deal about ourselves when we balance our energies. Attention is drawn to the areas that are out of balance and have caused problems in our lives. These areas typically contain some of our strongest soul energies. Balancing these areas gives us a chance to take a closer look at the soul energies that make us who we are.

> Areas that are out of balance typically contain some of our strongest soul energies.

Balancing our energy changes our lives. Suffering and pain are caused by imbalance. As the imbalances are brought into balance, suffering and pain decrease. Peace and harmony replace them. Since the integration process happens at the soul level, individuals first see changes in their personal lives. Then the changes become evident in the world around them. As we balance these energies within, we help to balance them for the world. It is part of the role we play in creating the balanced world of our dreams.

If the soul were to be compared to a piece of fabric, the various energy families would be analogous to the web of the fabric. Another set of energies makes up the woof, or cross fibers, of it. These are the masculine and feminine energies of the soul. Integrating our masculine and feminine sides is a critical component of balancing our energy. It is very difficult to live the life of our dreams, or have a balanced world, if these energies are not unified.

2. Integrate the Masculine and Feminine Sides

Our masculine and feminine sides are integrated into all the energy families. The masculine side is very good at utilizing the heavier energies of the energy families to help us exist and support ourselves in physicality. The feminine side utilizes the lighter energies, helping us to connect with each other and our spiritual selves. The simplified web and woof diagram given below may help you to visualize how they are interwoven with the energy families. In reality, the interweaving occurs multidimensionally.

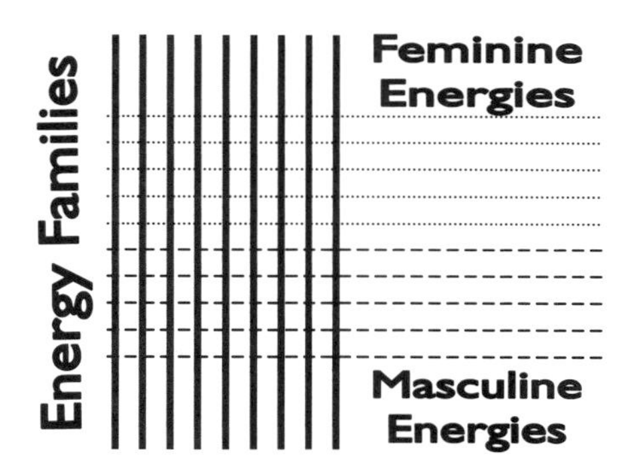

The masculine and feminine energies tend to work in pairs. They complement and support one another. If one constituent of the energy pair is disowned, the other will become ineffective, out of line, or corrupt. For example, if Bill has disowned the feminine part of himself that contains the vision for his soul, the masculine aspect that carries out that vision will not be balanced. It may run rampant, being driven by the ego. Or it may go into hiding, causing him to "fail" at his endeavors.

When we disown any part of our masculine and feminine sides, or when we deny part of an energy family, we tear holes in the fabric of our souls. This creates a feeling of being incomplete. It prevents us from fully utilizing all of our gifts

When we disown any part of our masculine and feminine sides, or when we deny part of an energy family, we tear holes in the fabric of our souls.

and abilities. And it puts us in a state of imbalance. You worked on reweaving various parts of your energy families in the last section. This section will help you to reweave and balance the masculine and feminine sides.

The masculine and feminine sides have been out of balance both within ourselves personally and "outside" ourselves in the world at large. All of us have both a masculine side and a feminine side. Most of us have denied various parts of each.

Where Are the Holes?

The way we view each gender in physical life can tell us a lot about the condition of our masculine and feminine sides. It is a mirror to the way we feel about those aspects of ourselves. The following questions may help you to discover the holes in the masculine and feminine threads of your soul. Your answers will give you clues as to which parts of yourself you have judged, rejected, or denied.

1. What kinds of derogatory statements have you heard yourself say about either gender?
2. What behaviors cause you to disrespect one gender or the other?
3. At times, do you ever wish you were the opposite gender? Why?
4. Do you prefer to be with or have friends of a particular gender? Why?
5. What causes you to distrust the other gender?
6. What negative feelings arise when you think of each gender? What about them brings up these feelings?

When we put down, disparage, or judge another for *anything*, we are judging that same exact thing in ourselves. Whatever we are still judging in others, we have not healed or integrated in ourselves. When we have healed and balanced our own inner selves, we then have compassion for others' states of being, no matter what they look like. We don't need to condone it, but we will allow them to have their experience.

It is virtually impossible to create the life of our dreams if we have not healed, balanced, and integrated our masculine and feminine sides. The qualities, gifts, and attributes of both are required to manifest the desires and needs of the soul on earth. What does each side bring to the table?

The Masculine Side

Let's begin with the masculine side. We are more familiar with how it works because it has been the stronger side in our world. The masculine side helps us to survive. It knows how to provide for us and get things done on this physical plane. It is good at thinking logically and rationally. It achieves goals by laying out the logical steps required and focusing on their accomplishment. It protects us and sets our boundaries. It watches out for us and covers our backs. Our masculine side is strong, capable, and down to earth. The masculine side knows how to use the denser energies to make things work on the physical plane.

The masculine side knows how to use the denser energies to make things work on the physical plane.

These are all wonderful attributes, and quite necessary to living a happy and successful life on earth. Why, then, does the masculine side sometimes get such a bad rap? It is because, when the masculine side takes over and is not balanced by the feminine side, the physical part of life becomes all-important. Life tends to be directed by the ego. The masculine side calls upon the dark energies to help it accomplish the goals set by the ego. These goals can be harmful to the self or others. Life can become stressful and busy. One may have everything he or she could ever want materially, but be lacking in personal fulfillment or in meaningful relationships.

The dark energies used to accomplish the ego's agenda may include greed, control, competition, injustice, rigidity, and intolerance. When out of balance, these energies can lead to war, pillage, abuse, rape, murder, totalitarianism, oppression, economic rifts and social caste systems. These conditions are not unfamiliar to us.

I caution you *not* to think of these as traits of men. They are traits of an overly dominant masculine side in *both* men and women. They have also been traits of our world in places where the masculine energy has dominated the feminine energy. An overly dominant masculine side can be one's shadow side. It may sabotage one's attempts to speak and live one's truth, fulfill one's soul purpose, or collaborate with others for the highest good of all.

The Feminine Side

Let us turn now to the feminine energies. There may not be quite as much familiarity with the feminine attributes and imbalances as with those of the masculine. The feminine side knows how to work with the lighter energies to connect the physical with the spiritual. It gives us beauty, compassion, vision, gentleness, kindness, caring, unity, and expansiveness. We all have this side. As with the masculine side, it may be submerged or hidden to some extent. In some, it is far more evident.

> The feminine side knows how to work with the lighter energies to connect the physical with the spiritual.

When the feminine side runs rampant and is not balanced by the masculine side, it becomes very difficult to live a physical life. There is a tendency toward anarchy, flightiness, ungroundedness, hallucination, the neglect of self, the inability to support oneself, instability, homelessness, and irrational thoughts and behaviors. One may have wonderfully supportive relationships, but be unable to provide food, clothing, and shelter for the family. One may have lofty visions for his or her life, but be unable to bring them into reality. These are *not* the traits of women. They are the traits of an overly dominant feminine side in *both* men and women. An overly dominant feminine side can be one's shadow side. It may sabotage one's attempts to support oneself, live a productive life, fulfill one's soul purpose, stay grounded, or work through problems.

Competition Between the Masculine and Feminine

Our masculine and feminine sides have been in competition for a very long time. There is much evidence of this in the world. It comes through in the beliefs and actions that support the idea that one sex is "better" than the other. These include such things as sexual discrimination, sexual harassment, sexual favors, disdain for babies of a certain gender, and the control, manipulation, and abuse of one sex over the other. Our outer world is merely a reflection of our inner selves.

Internally, our masculine and feminine sides often have difficulty coming to grips with their equality. They tend to resist balance and integration. The feminine side may be afraid of being bullied by the masculine side. The masculine side may be afraid of losing control or not being able to survive should the feminine side become too strong. One's personal fears must be healed in order for these two sides to come together. The abilities of both are required for the creation of the life of our dreams.

> Internally, our masculine and feminine sides often have difficulty coming to grips with their equality.

Benefits of Integrating the Masculine and Feminine Sides

The following visual experience might help you to understand the benefits of integrating your masculine and feminine sides. It was given to a very good friend of mine as we worked on integrating our own masculine and feminine sides. She saw a fish tank that was divided down the middle. One side of the tank contained the fragile beauty of a salt water system. It was filled with colorful fish, sea anemones, and coral. Its otherworldly beauty was spectacular. The other side of the tank contained a stable fresh water system. The fish, tadpoles, and plants were all shades of browns and greens. Its earthly stability felt comforting and secure. The fish and plants on each side of the divider felt safe in their own environment. They felt that it was the only environment in which they could survive.

Then a very interesting thing happened. The divider was removed. The salt water and fresh water began to mix. The fish expanded their horizons, now having the whole tank in which to explore and move around. The environment gently melded together into one that was both beautiful and stable. None of the fish or plants was harmed. In fact, they thrived. The fresh water fish loved the greater beauty. The salt-water fish loved the greater stability. The green of the plants was enhanced against the backdrop of coral. All lived in harmony, appreciating how their lives had been improved by the attributes and gifts of the other side.

> When we integrate our masculine and feminine sides, we thrive in the stability provided by the masculine side and the beauty imparted by the feminine side.

This is what happens when we integrate our masculine and feminine sides. We thrive in the stability provided by the masculine side and the beauty imparted by the feminine side. Our lives are greatly improved. We take advantage of the gifts and abilities of both. Both are needed to create the life of our dreams. That life looks and feels much better and far different from the life where the masculine and feminine are separated. We are able to set a vision for our lives and carry the vision through. Each person has the desire and ability to get in touch with and develop his or her inner spiritual self. At the same time, the physical needs of all are met. At the personal level, life becomes much easier as the gifts of both are fully utilized.

At the global level, balancing the masculine energy with more feminine energy would go a long way toward creating a world where people live together in peace, harmony, and freedom. We would see a world where men and women were treated as equals. Both would be honored, respected, and commended for their gifts and abilities. They would learn how to work together through collaboration rather than competition. Domestic violence, the glass ceiling, and sexual harassment could be things of the past.

We don't have to wait for everyone in the world to integrate his or her masculine and feminine sides, in order to have such a life. By doing so ourselves, we each create this kind of personal environment. When we are integrated and balanced within, we draw people and situations into our lives that support the change. Our outer world always mirrors and reflects our inner condition.

Our outer world always mirrors and reflects our inner condition.

The Role of the Brain

The separation and imbalance of our masculine and feminine sides is due in part to the fact that the brain is separated into right and left hemispheres. The two hemispheres don't always work well together. One side of the brain tends to dominate the other. This results in an imbalance in the coordinated and collaborative use of the masculine and feminine sides. The dominant half filters out much of the information that is received; dictates the directions, goals, and activities of the person's life; and causes imbalance.

The left hemisphere controls the right side of the body, gives us the abilities to communicate in language and think logically and linearly, and helps us to "do" things in a logical and progressive sequence. It is our "doing" and "giving" side. Generally, the right side of the body and the left side of the brain are said to be one's masculine side. If the left hemisphere is overly dominant, the individual may be logical and practical, but not be very creative or expansive in his or her thinking. He or she may be very good at doing things for others, but not be very good at self-nurturing.

Generally, the right side of the body and the left side of the brain are said to be one's masculine side.

The right hemisphere controls the left side of the body and gives us the ability to envision and create. It is our "being" and "receiving" side. Generally, the left side of the body and the right side of the brain are said to be one's feminine side. An individual with an overly dominant right brain will tend to be very creative and expansive in his or her thinking, but not very logical or practical. He or she may be very good at smelling the roses, but not very good at earning the money to buy them. We are meant to be both. We are capable of being both. Both are needed to have a balanced perspective and to live the balanced life of our dreams.

Generally, the left side of the body and the right side of the brain are said to be one's feminine side.

Update the Operating System

How do we merge our masculine and feminine sides? How do we bring them forth and get them to work together? Using the analogy of rebooting a computer, we must "reboot our minds" so that the two halves work together. But before we can do this, we must first update our operating systems.

Our operating systems are the beliefs by which we live. We have many outdated beliefs that keep us separate. Some of them have to do with the separation of male and female. Others have to do with the separation of ourselves from each other and All That Is. We must update the operating system by updating these beliefs to support unity consciousness. This will promote the integration of our masculine and feminine sides. What might be some of the updates called for?

Updating Our Operating Systems

Old Beliefs	Updated Beliefs
The masculine and feminine are not equal	The masculine and feminine are different and equal
Competition is necessary for survival	Collaboration is the foundation for the life of our dreams
Control keeps things in order	Freedom produces order naturally
Separation keeps us safe	Unity keeps us strong
We are what we do	Our doing proceeds from our being
The best defense is a good offense	Being defensive *is* being offensive
We are separate	We are One in our uniqueness

I have seen intuitively that many of these beliefs are stored energetically in the membrane that separates the right and left sides of the brain. It separates the two halves and keeps them in competition. By updating the operating system (our beliefs), and then rebooting the mind, we transform the energetic membrane to allow both halves to work together in collaboration. It is analogous to removing the wall between the two halves of the aquarium. You may use the following exercises to help you do this.

Exercise – Updating Your Operating System

1. *Ground yourself to the earth and your Higher Self.*
2. *Focus your thoughts on one gender, then the other. Are there any negative emotions elicited about each gender? Write them down. The table below gives you a method for recording your answers. It also provides some examples.*
3. *Ask your Higher Self to reveal to you any prejudiced beliefs that are keeping these emotions in place. These beliefs are keeping your masculine and feminine sides separate and in competition.*
4. *Now ask your Higher Self to give you new beliefs that are honoring to the masculine and feminine.*

Example

Sex	Emotion	Prejudice	New Belief
M	Disrespect	Men are selfish	The masculine part of me helps me to set appropriate boundaries
F	Disdain	Women have a know-it-all attitude	The feminine part of me provides vision for my life
M	Condescension	Men are opinionated and narrow-minded	The masculine part of me keeps me focused and on task
F	Disregard	Women are too soft to be good managers	The feminine part of me gives me compassion for myself and others

Exercise - Rebooting the Mind

1. *While remaining grounded, set the intention for the new beliefs obtained in the previous exercise to replace the old beliefs that separated your masculine and feminine sides. Intend that they be installed and integrated all the way down to the DNA and soul levels.*
2. *Picture these beliefs transforming the membrane that separates the right and left hemispheres of the brain into a super-switchboard. It connects and unifies the corresponding cells of each half of the brain.*
3. *Imagine your masculine and feminine sides, and the right and left sides of your brain, working together in collaboration, with complete respect for the gifts and abilities of each.*

Much of this updating and rebooting occurs when the individual is ready to open the third eye. The third eye provides the balanced and integrated perspective of the soul. It is difficult for the mind to "receive" such a balanced perspective if it is still working under the old paradigm of separation and competition. The more the right and left sides of the brain work in collaboration and equality, the more accurate and undistorted will be the pictures that are received from the soul.

As our energy families and our masculine and feminine sides come into balance, we become more expanded and balanced in our perspective on things. This helps us to receive a clearer vision for our lives—one that is more in line with the soul's purpose.

The third eye relies on the information obtained from the other chakras to provide us with a complete and balanced picture. There are things we can do to enhance this transfer of information. One of these is to heal and open each chakra. The other is to balance the energies of the chakras with each other.

Each chapter in this book was designed to help you heal and open a particular chakra or portal. The next section will help you to balance the energies of the chakras with each other. This helps them to work together to create a vision for your life and bring it into reality.

3. Balancing the Chakras

Sometimes the energy flow between the chakras gets out of balance. This happens when one or more chakras become constricted, or closed. The ones that are more open have a greater amount of energy passing through them than do the more closed ones. (The terms "open" and "closed" are relative. It would be rare for a chakra to be completely closed, and there is no limit to the openness of a chakra.) Balancing the chakras evens out the flow of energy throughout the body. Closed chakras can cause the chi to stagnate in our bodies. One or more closed chakras will cause our internal energy to become imbalanced. This can make us feel out of sorts, cause physical problems, and limit the flow of information to the sixth chakra.

The chakras are affected not only by our own energy, but also by the energy of others. They open and close depending upon what we are thinking and feeling, and how we are responding to the people and circumstances around us. When they are closed, we may feel withdrawn, heavy-hearted, and disconnected. When they are open, we usually feel light, expanded and connected.

> Opening and balancing the chakras helps the mind, body, emotions, and soul to work together in harmony.

Opening and balancing the chakras helps the mind, body, emotions and soul to work together in harmony, and maximizes the use of our chi. It is soothing and centering, and a wonderful way to start the day, prepare for meditation, or access one's guidance. There are various ways to open and balance the energy between the chakras. Several methods are given below. You may wish to experiment with them to see what works best for you.

Sound

One way to open and balance the chakras is through sound. The chakras are very responsive to sound. There are music CD's available that contain certain vibrational sounds for each of the chakras. There are also Tibetan Bowls of different sizes that emit tones for particular chakras. These are helpful for opening the chakras.

Toning and chanting are other methods used to open and balance the chakras. Both use the voice. Since the sound comes from within, toning and chanting are very effective in moving energy in the body. In toning, a particular note is held on a vowel sound, such as "ah" or "om". The vowel sound used varies with the chakra. This can be done in groups or individually, with or without certain intent.

Chanting is similar to toning, but words are used, and there may be more rhythm and melody. Words from one's own native language can be used with intent. Words might spontaneously come forth from one's inner self. In that case, they might not be from a language that one consciously recognizes. Systematically chanting through the chakras is a good way to open and balance them. The words strengthen the intent. Additional light can be introduced into each chakra, helping to open it, by visualizing the color of the chakra.[1]

Visualization

The chakras may also be opened and balanced using visualization. Keep in mind that it is not the *technique* that opens them, as much as the *intent*. You can create your own

---

[1] Chanting and toning exercises may be found at www.bridgesofunity.com

visualization that helps you focus your awareness on your chakras. Or you might try the following visualization, which was developed by my brother, Robert J. Lins, M.D.

Exercise – Visualization to Open and Balance the Chakras

1. *Ground yourself. Breath fully and slowly. Set your intent on opening and balancing your chakras.*
2. *Begin with the first chakra, located at the base of your spine. Imagine a cylinder of energy, about the size of a large oatmeal box, extending through your body from front to back, at the location of the first chakra. The cylinder extends into your aura both in front and behind.*
3. *Picture a continuous shaft of warm love-light entering the front of the cylinder of energy, filling it with love energy. Take several deep breaths as you visualize the love-light energy filling and opening your first chakra, expanding it out into your aura and beyond.*
4. *Feel your chakra expanding into your body, filling the sacral area of your body, your legs, and feet, with its energy.*
5. *Take several breaths as the chakra energy expands, and then move on to the next chakra.*
6. *Repeat steps two through five for each of the remaining chakras, beginning with the second chakra, and ending with the seventh chakra. Imagine the chakra expanding into the body immediately surrounding it.*
7. *When the seventh chakra has been opened, and while still grounded, imagine the shaft of love-light energy coming in the crown of your head, all the way through your body, and into the earth. This will synchronize and balance the energies of the chakras with each other as it flows down your spine. Continue with this intent, breathing with awareness (to keep you in the moment) for as long as you like.*

Hand Movements

Some people have trouble visualizing, but desire to have a "silent" way of opening the chakras. Here is a third method, which you can do on yourself, or on another person. It uses hand movements to deepen the intent of opening and balancing the chakras. I use this technique on my clients during their bodywork sessions.

Exercise – Opening and Balancing the Chakras Using Hand Movements

1. *Ground yourself. Set your intent on opening and balancing the chakras. (If working on another person, have him or her ground as well, and lie down, if possible).*
2. *Begin with the first chakra. Make broad sweeping circles with both hands three to twelve inches over the front or back of the body, between the feet and the base of the spine. Intend that the first chakra open and expand through the body and aura. Continue making these circles until the energy in this area feels strong.*
3. *When the first chakra feels open to you, move one hand to the second chakra, making circles in the area of the lower abdomen. Continue making circles with the other hand over the first chakra at the base of the spine. (You don't need to extend the first circle to the feet anymore. Instead, center it over the perineum). This helps to balance and smooth the energy between the two chakras. Keep on making circles with both hands over the first and second chakras until the energy of the second chakra feels stronger, and the first chakra feels "complete". This will be an intuitive knowing, or a tingling sensation in the hands. You can ask your Higher Self for a sense of awareness regarding when it is time to move to the next chakra.*
4. *Move your hands to the second and third chakras, making circles over them, until you are guided to move again. Continue up the seven chakras in this fashion.*

Exercise (cont.)

5. *There are chakras beyond the seventh chakra. Energy flows through these from the Higher Self. While one hand is still circling the seventh chakra, circle with the other hand about 18 inches beyond the top of the head. As you do this, intend that these chakras open up to the energy of the Higher Self (or if doing it on another person, from the other person's Higher Self).*
6. *When they feel "complete", move your hands another 18 inches above the head, to the next chakra. (The hand farthest from the body is now approximately 36 inches above the head).*
7. *When this feels complete, intend to balance the energy between the chakras. Move your hands over the whole length of the body, from above the head, to the feet, and back again. Intend that the love energy from the Higher Self fill and balance the chakras and body. The energy flows from the Higher Self, through the body and aura, to earth and back again. Do this several times. End with a movement from the head to the feet. Then hold the feet to ground them for as long as you like.*

Balancing our chakras, energy families, and masculine and feminine sides, feels wonderful. As you balance yourself internally, you will create balance in your life. Your relationships will improve. Your emotions will stabilize. Your body will feel better. Your mind will be clearer. You will experience more peace, harmony, honor, and abundance. Balancing one's energy is life changing. As you balance yourself on the inside, you will create the life of your dreams on the outside.

Signs of the Portal Opening

The opening of the third eye is accompanied by major shifts in our consciousness. Do you seem to be more intuitive or psychic than you used to be? Has your sense of time changed? Are your dreams more vivid and real? These are all indications that your third eye is opening.

There are more signs pointing to the opening of the sixth chakra than with any other chakra. Information begins to pour in from the Higher Self. Some of this is information that you are to bring to the world as part of your purpose. You might receive unusual insights regarding a particular aspect of life. You might discover a new way of doing things.

Other information will assist you in your personal life. You will begin to see life from a different perspective—one that is more open, compassionate, wise, and expanded. You will see through the illusions and manipulations created by others. You will see through the illusions you have accepted as "just part of life". You will gain a renewed passion for following your truth. The past and present circumstances and events of your life will make more sense.

Your sense of time and space may begin to be altered. Time may seem to expand or contract into timelessness. You might have a sense of multiple existences and parallel lives. Dreamtime may be filled with scenes of another life. You might dream of loved ones who are deceased or carry on a life you started with a presently divorced spouse. The dreams may seem more real. You might continue your dreams even after you awaken, merging dreamtime into your present life.

Your psychic and intuitive powers may become stronger. You might know or sense things before they actually happen or prior to being informed of them. You may receive messages in your dreams. You might see things through your third eye that are not perceived by the physical eyes. It may at times seem as if you are looking into another dimension or time.

Do not be frightened by these things. You are not going crazy. They may seem abnormal to us because our third eyes have been closed for so long. They are completely normal.

We are also undergoing many changes in our bodies. The sixth chakra receives its information from, and therefore works closely with, all the other chakras. As the sixth chakra opens, whatever is yet to be healed in the other chakras comes to the forefront to be addressed. This is one reason why the opening and healing of the chakras is done in order from the first to the seventh. It is much easier on us and on our bodies.

The Higher Self may choose to work on the chakras one by one, or it may heal multiple chakras at the same time. You may experience more of the temporary physical discomforts and unusual symptoms associated with the opening of the sixth chakra than with any other. It may at times feel as if you are falling apart or "getting old before your time", because it affects so much of the body. Rest assured, you are not falling apart. You are falling together. Many changes in the body are made as the system is "rebooted". It is as if the body is being "rewired" to reroute the flow of information into the sixth chakra and to accommodate a higher level of energy and consciousness.

Rest assured, you are not falling apart. You are falling together.

The next page contains a partial list of symptoms that others and I myself have temporarily experienced during the opening of the sixth chakra. They don't all appear at once, but rather tend to appear one to three at a time. Yours may be similar, or they may be different. Many of them resemble flu-like symptoms. The Higher Self can do a great deal of work on the body when one is down in bed with the "flu".

Symptoms During the Opening of the Sixth Chakra[2]

1. Headaches
2. Achiness
3. Neck and shoulder pain
4. A feeling of "disconnection" between the head and the body
5. Pain in the occipital and surface areas of the skull
6. Arm, hand, or wrist pain and tendonitis
7. Twitching in the eye(s)
8. Pain in or behind the eyes
9. Sensations and/or ringing in the ear(s)
10. Pain and tenderness in the jaws, masseter muscles, gums, and/or teeth
11. Sinus and/or lung congestion
12. Heart arrhythmia
13. Breast and nipple tenderness
14. Digestive problems
15. Tightness and tenderness in the hips, iliac crest, and legs
16. Sore feet
17. Diminished ability of one or more of the senses
18. Extreme tiredness
19. Increased sensitivity to certain foods and toxins
20. Poor body temperature control
21. Lucid dreaming
22. Insomnia
23. Mental fogginess
24. Emotional fluctuations

---

[2] For a more detailed explanation of these symptoms and their causes, please visit www.bridgesofunity.com.

This is quite a list. No wonder it sometimes feels as if we are falling apart! Although the symptoms associated with the opening of our chakras may be uncomfortable, they are only temporary, and need not be a cause for alarm. They allow us to focus in on the areas that are being healed. This helps us to set a stronger intention for the healing to take place.

The symptoms often affect one side of the body at a time. When this occurs, it usually means that the work being done is related to either the masculine or the feminine side. I am right-handed, a writer, and a former engineer, so it is not surprising that the dominant left side of my brain would be the first to resist the integration of my masculine and feminine sides, causing sensations and pain in the right side of my body.

The left side of my body followed suit after the symptoms in the right side subsided. The physical symptoms then went back and forth between my right and left sides until they were integrated. It may feel like you're being a hypochondriac. You are not. It is all part of the changes being made in the body and the fine-tuning of the balancing process. Stick with it.

There may be times when you feel on top of the world, followed by other times when you feel like you're back at square one. There may be mood swings, joy-filled days, and feelings of depression. There may be times when you feel fully loved and loving, and other times when you feel angry and isolated. (And you thought it was all hormonal!) There may be times of unimaginable growth and insights, and other times of waiting. It is all part of the process.

Much of the time, physical and emotional discomforts are simply the result of physical and energetic changes being made. These are growth pains. We are going through a birthing process. There may be no medical explanation for them. You can ask your Higher Self whether the symptoms are purely energetic, related to the opening of your third eye, due to something that may require medical attention, or a combination of the above.

The symptoms oftentimes come in waves—sometimes worse, sometimes better—until they disappear completely. They may come and go, lasting anywhere from a few minutes to a few months at a time. We can ask for assistance from our Higher Selves and healing guides, if desired. It helps to set the intention before bedtime that the transition be accomplished during sleep at a rate that the body can easily handle. It may take some time, so be patient. We are healing in amazing ways.

Sometimes there are issues to be addressed. Ask your Higher Self to inform you whether there are issues behind the symptoms. Ask if there are any behavior or belief patterns that need to be changed in order for the integration to occur. Addressing the issues and balancing the corresponding energies can reduce the intensity and longevity of the symptoms. The transition may go more smoothly as the resistance to it is decreased.

Be aware of foods that may aggravate the physical symptoms. The body can temporarily become very sensitive to certain foods and toxins that interfere with the integration process or that lower the body's energy level. For the time being, reduce or eliminate foods that cause you discomfort. A healthy diet and exercise go a long way toward helping us to feel better at any stage in our lives.

You may find that certain techniques for moving stuck energy can help to reduce the symptoms. I found massage, cranial sacral therapy, meditation, and salt baths to be particularly helpful. It is quite normal to feel tired. The body is undergoing many changes and needs its sleep. Your normal sleep cycles may be disrupted. Napping during the day can help to give your body its much-needed rest.

If you have the desire to do something creative, by all means do it. The sixth chakra is directly connected to the second chakra. Exercising the creative energy from the second chakra helps to open the third eye. It also helps to strengthen the right half of the brain so that it may be more fully integrated with the left side of the brain.

The Balanced Life

All of the discomfort and strange sensations become worth it when we see the changes it brings to our lives and the world. How does balancing our energies enhance our lives? What difference does it make to the world?

First the world in our immediate sphere of existence changes—the ways we interact with others, the harmony we feel, and the circumstances that surround us. Our relationships become more harmonious. They are based on honor of self and others. Our differences are respected. There is no more distinctly "right way" and "wrong way".

We see things from multiple perspectives. This allows us to get a clearer picture of whatever topic or idea we are exploring. We are able to accept the fact that two "opposing" ideas are really two perspectives of the same picture (like viewing a mountain range from different sides). We are able to explore ideas more completely through open discussion. The tendency is to merge perspectives, like pieces of a jigsaw puzzle.

Competitive tendencies decrease. We begin to work in collaboration—acknowledging, honoring, and embracing the individual gifts that we have. Each person's gifts and abilities are emphasized and revered in support of the whole.

There are no more "cookie cutter" personality profiles required to "fit in" with a certain school, society, institution, or corporate culture. The false unity of sameness that has been demanded in the past is replaced by an insistence that the uniqueness of the individual be tantamount. We understand that the whole group suffers, and is incomplete, if each person's gifts and abilities are not fully utilized.

Our perception of the world changes as we change ourselves. A loving, compassionate, and respectful world shows up when we learn to have love, compassion and respect for ourselves. Peace surrounds us when we find peace within. Abundance flows all around us when we allow it to flow through us.

The effects of balancing our energy go far beyond the borders of our lives. As more and more people balance their energies, the world at large will go through a major change. It will become the world of our dreams: a place of unconditional love, of global peace, and true abundance. All countries will work together in collaboration for the highest good of all. There will be acceptance of all cultural, ethnic, and religious differences. Governments will promote the well being of the whole before those of special interest groups. Schools, businesses, corporations, and other organizations will encourage the creativity and personal fulfillment of the individual. The earth, and all that it sustains, will be nurtured and cared for.

Healing ourselves is without question the most important thing that we can do to bring healing to our planet. Balancing our own energy is essential if we are to have a balanced world. As we each do our part, the world will again emerge in all its radiant splendor and beauty. This was the state of the "Garden of Eden", and we are bringing it back.

The Inspired Life

As the right and left hemispheres of the brain become balanced and integrated, inspiration comes in more easily through the seventh, or crown chakra—the subject of the next chapter. This information may be of a creative nature, may be purely informative, or may be guidance needed to live one's daily life. This is essential for creating and living the life of our dreams. It helps in making decisions that support one's path. It helps to eliminate the struggle, stress, and fear of not knowing, or of making the wrong decision.

Throughout this chapter you have been encouraged to ask your Higher Self to provide you with information regarding your healing process. Maybe you inquired about underlying issues and beliefs. Perhaps you asked whether your physical symptoms would benefit from medical attention. How did that go? Were you able to get some answers? Or were you met with silence, uncertainty, or confusion?

Have there been occasions in your life when you wished you had a magic ball to give you answers to your questions? Wouldn't it be nice to have a direct line with some source of knowledge to guide us through the changes in our lives? Sometimes it seems so difficult to get the answers and guidance we desire. And then when we do get answers, we're not always sure of the source. How do we know that we're not just "making it up", or that the ego, or some mysterious force, hasn't interjected its own agenda?

These are very real questions and concerns that most people have. I have struggled with them myself. As your third eye opens, you will begin to see a wonderful vision for your life. Wouldn't it be great to have a personal guide to show you how to make that vision a reality? It would make life so much easier.

The fact is, you *do* have a personal guide. It is your Higher Self. In the next chapter, you will learn how to access the guidance of your Higher Self through your crown chakra. You will be given specific techniques to obtain answers to all the hundreds of questions that arise in your daily life. You will learn how to tell the difference between the voice of your Higher Self and the voice of your ego or some outside influence. By opening the seventh portal to your soul, you will be able to access the guidance of your Higher Self so that you can create the life of your dreams with confidence and ease.

welcome to

THE SEVENTH PORTAL

to your soul...

The Seventh Portal

Name	Seventh or Crown Chakra
Location	Top of the head
Traditional Color	Violet-white
Functions	• Accesses light and energy from the Universe • Receives wisdom, guidance and information from the Higher Self
Balanced Tendencies	Feeling of connection with All That Is; spiritual awakening and wisdom; understanding of the deep mysteries of life; knowing; clarity of thought; spirit-guided in the present moment; inspiration; insight; unity consciousness; non-attachment
Unbalanced Tendencies	Feeling of separation from All That Is; controlled by the ego and mind; tendency to over-plan or procrastinate; blind acceptance of authority and the beliefs and ideas of others
Physical Problems	Neuro-muscular , skeletal and skin diseases; chronic exhaustion not associated with physical ailments, sensitivity to light, sound, environment
Mental and Emotional Issues	Confusing inner voices; mind chatter; racing thoughts; scattered focus; given to fantasy; indecisive; driven; idealistic
Restoring Validations	I am one with All That Is. I trust the guidance of my Higher Self. I desire the best and highest good of all. I am responsible for the direction of my life. I am open to new information and possibilities.

PORTAL #7

Live With Ease by Accessing Your Guidance

He was a delivery route driver—had been for years. The day began like any other, making deliveries of packaged pastries to the local grocery and convenience stores. It was late morning. He was cruising down the highway on the way to his final stop before lunchtime. The day had gone well. He was right on schedule. But schedules are subject to change. On this particular day, something happened that altered the schedule of his whole life.

He couldn't believe what he was seeing. The dry desert terrain of the Southwestern United States that he knew so well began to transform into images of Egypt. It was as if he had been transported to another time and place. He thought he was hallucinating. Quickly, he pulled over to the side of the road and stopped. Three balls of light entered the cab of the truck and began to speak to him. He was shocked by the sight of them, but even more shocked by what they had to say. They told him that a few miles down the road, he would have an accident and be killed. This was the designated time for him, according to the contracts created prior to his birth.

Following that shocking news, the voices of light told him that his services were needed in other ways. He was asked to make a decision.

He could choose to abide by his original contract, ending his life on earth. Or he could write a new contract, which would extend his life. Under the new contract, he would become an artist, tapping into abilities that even he didn't know he had. His art would be used to heal others. He would receive visions of the designs and record them on paper and canvas. This was indeed a life-or-death decision. Without hesitation, he chose the new contract in artistic service to the world. He had no idea how it would happen. But somehow, he knew it would.

This is a true story. Things like this really do happen. People receive guidance in all kinds of miraculous, supernatural ways—guidance so obvious that it can't possibly be missed. But for most of us, guidance comes in much more subtle ways—ways that can easily be missed.

Guidance does not need to be an extraordinary happening. In fact, most of the time, it is quite ordinary. Guidance is not a once in a lifetime event. Guidance occurs moment by moment. But we must be tuned to it if we are to hear it. We must know what it sounds like and feels like. And we must know how to tell the difference between true guidance and misguidance.

Are you having difficulty accessing your guidance? Do you depend on others to tell you what to do? Is your life in gridlock because you simply don't know the next step to take? Are you afraid of ruining your life by making the wrong decision? Have you been feeling that you are being called to make some changes in your life, but don't know where to start? These are common concerns.

Many people have told me that they feel a change coming in their lives. Some don't know what the change is. Most don't know how to make it happen. Trying to make decisions involving change for one's life can be difficult and confusing.

This chapter will help you to sort through the confusion. It will show you how to gain clarity by accessing your inner guidance. You will learn how to tell the subtle differences between the true voice of your Higher Self and the false voices that may mislead you. You will understand why you are sometimes given multiple answers, or no answer at all, and what to do about it. And you will be given ways to get concrete answers to your specific questions.

This chapter will help you to open the seventh portal to your soul, which is your crown chakra, located at the top of your head. The crown chakra is our information highway. It is located close to the brain for this very reason. Through this portal, we have access to the wisdom of the Universe. It is the pathway through which we receive light, energy, information, and guidance from the Higher Self. The more we exercise our intuitive abilities, the more open this channel becomes. The more we learn to consult and depend on our guidance for direction and answers, the easier life becomes.

The crown chakra is our information highway. Through this portal we access the wisdom of the Universe.

It is not necessary to worry and fret about the future. It is not necessary to plan out every detail. It is not necessary to create such stress in our lives. Our Higher Selves are waiting for us to ask for their help. They are there to give us the guidance and answers we need to live the life of our dreams. They are there to help us fulfill the divine plan for our lives, day by day. They are there to help us make things happen with synchronicity so that we can live our lives with ease.

True Guidance

True guidance comes from the Higher Self. The Higher Self is that part of one's spirit that resides in the higher dimensions. It is the link between the soul and the Universe. Because the Higher Self resides in the higher dimensions, it is less susceptible to the illusions and distortions that we hold to be "true" in the third dimension. That is why it is important to connect with the Higher Self when seeking guidance.

Not all of the information that comes through the crown chakra is from one's Higher Self. Much of it is from other sources, many of which contain the distortions and illusions of the lower dimensions. We are similar to satellite dishes that receive input from many different channels. Psychics and Intuitives use this pathway when they do readings by "tuning in" to the energy of another. We all have that capability. It is possible to get a message from one's Higher Self one moment, and from another source the next. If we don't know how to differentiate between the voice of the Higher Self and the other voices, we may end up following the wrong voice.

We are similar to satellite dishes that receive input from many different channels.

These voices are like radio signals. Trying to tune in to a weak radio signal can be difficult. The signal is garbled because of the overlap in signals. It is sometimes even possible to hear two stations at the same time. Unless we are familiar with the sound of the station for which we are seeking, we might tune in to the wrong station, or get mixed signals. The same is true when we are seeking guidance from the Higher Self.

Knowing how to hone in on our personal signal provides us with more accurate information. Opening the crown chakra gives us stronger signals. These are two aspects of receiving true and clear guidance. This chapter will help you to do both.

The Role of Guidance

Before we get into the specifics of accessing our guidance, let us take a moment to discuss its purpose. What is the role of guidance in our lives? Does it work even when we are not aware of it? Is life "preordained", or do we have conscious control over its outcome?"

I believe that the soul has an agenda for its physical life that is created prior to birth. The soul's agenda helps the soul to know who it is. It has certain lessons to learn, specific healing to accomplish, and distinct knowledge, accomplishments, and energies that it is to provide to the earth and those who live here. This is the divine plan for one's life. The fulfillment of it is the main reason why we are here. The divine plan encompasses a whole series of happenings throughout one's lifetime. It does not necessarily contain a culminating "big event". It may look quite ordinary on the surface. But underneath, extraordinary things are happening.

Because the soul lives in the density of our bodies and the distortions of the third dimension, it tends to "forget" what it came here to do. It is not unlike a puppy that goes outside to do its duty and ends up exploring the yard or digging in the dirt instead. So, like the puppy's master, the Higher Self, which resides outside the density of this dimension, reminds the soul of its responsibility. It knows what the soul is here to do and, as much as it can, sees to it that the job gets done.

It is not a "perfect" system, because we do have free will. We can choose to listen to and follow our guidance, or we can choose to follow a different path. Either one may be quite OK, for all of it is experience as far as the Universe is concerned. There really are no wrong turns. But for matters of high priority related to the soul's agenda, the Higher Self can get rather insistent. It can take out the proverbial two by four to get us to open our eyes to the path it is trying to get us to take. This can be a

We can choose to listen to and follow our guidance, or we can choose to follow a different path.

supernatural event, such as that of the truck driver. Or it can be a "forced" change, such as being fired from a job.

Let's return to the truck driver. What happened to him? He was glad to be alive. But it felt like his whole life had been turned upside down. He wondered, "How will this change come to pass? I am no artist. How do I get started? Who will buy my work? How am I to support myself?" Even with the clear-cut guidance he received, he was left with many unanswered questions and concerns.

Maybe you have experienced something like that yourself. Have you ever felt like you were clearly being nudged to do something, but you didn't know how to make it happen? Perhaps your mind told you it didn't make sense. Maybe you were afraid to make the change. So you didn't do it. Then, at a later date, perhaps it was forced upon you in some way. This sometimes happens when we are ready to make a shift in our lives—to a different job, a new relationship, or different surroundings. Something inside tells us that it is time for a change, but we ignore it. Then a situation occurs that forces the change. Out of the blue, a divorce, a fire, or an illness occurs that causes major changes.

Often, when we look back on it, we find that the change was for the best and we are much better off in some way. But it feels like suffering at the time. It is certainly possible for our Higher Selves to guide and direct our lives without our conscious awareness. In fact, it happens all the time, even in little things. But listening to and following our guidance can facilitate the changes needed in our lives with less suffering and more ease. And it certainly helps us to complete more of our soul's agenda for this lifetime.

Listening to and following our guidance can facilitate the changes needed in our lives with less suffering and more ease.

The truck driver received a grand vision for his life, but had no idea how the vision was to be accomplished. He was told to continue his daily routine until he received further instruction. Day after day went by. There were no more talking lights in his cab. The landscape was the same as always. Life seemed to go on as usual. Then one day he stopped at a truck stop and entered into conversation with another man. The conversation contained the guidance he needed to make the next step. It would easily have been missed had the truck driver not been looking for it.

The man told him of an organization that was helping people to heal their innermost fears, their physical problems, and their mental and emotional issues. The truck driver had an urge to contact them. He told them of his experience with the lights. They decided to work together. Since then, he has been getting visions of amazing new age artwork. They contain symbols and colors that help people to heal just by looking at them. Each piece serves a particular function. His art is being sold and distributed by this organization.

The role of guidance is to help us live life with greater ease and to accomplish the soul's agenda. Guidance can involve major changes in our lives, such as it did with the truck driver, or it can involve little everyday things. Our guidance can let us know what foods are good for us, when to purchase certain items, or how to spend our time each day. There is no question too large or too small to ask the Higher Self.

> The role of guidance is to help us live life with greater ease and to accomplish the soul's agenda.

Sometimes the soul's agenda can best be accomplished through a particular set of circumstances or with specific individuals. In those instances, we get a stronger leading from the Higher Self to do a particular thing. The soul may have contracts with various other souls to carry out and experience certain aspects of its divine plan. These souls are drawn to us at some point in our lives. The contracts may be with anyone—parents, children, siblings, partners, acquaintances, colleagues, friends, or passers-by.

Oftentimes the soul's agenda can be accomplished in any number of ways, with different people and circumstances. In those cases, the choice is ours to make. When we get no answer at all to a question, or have multiple options set before us with no clear-cut path to take, the decision we make may not be critical to the soul's agenda. Perhaps it can be accomplished through multiple means. Maybe the timing is not right for an immediate answer. We don't necessarily get clear and specific answers to our every question. But it never hurts to ask whether the Higher Self has a preference. I normally ask what would serve the best and highest good for myself and all concerned when making a decision.

Oftentimes the soul's agenda can be accomplished in any number of ways, with different people and circumstances.

Inner Voices

How do we receive guidance? The truck driver received guidance through the balls of light, and then through the conversation at the truck stop. There are many ways of receiving guidance, if we are open to them. The answers to our questions can come through a book, movie, or life occurrence. The important thing is to consciously ask the question and then to remain open to the answer, in whatever way it comes. Then it is important to test to see whether the answer resonates with the Higher Self.

Much of the time, guidance comes through an inner voice or feeling. But we need to be tuned into our feelings and the voice of the Higher Self if we are to receive accurate guidance. The mind can be so full of extraneous thoughts and voices that it may be difficult to sort through them.

Can you think of a time when it felt like there were multiple voices inside you telling you what to do? One voice may have said, "Take this path". While another said, "No, take that one". A third cautioned, "Don't do anything". It can be confusing. Not all of the voices that speak to us from within are of the Higher Self. If there seems to be a conflict of interest going on internally, you can be fairly certain that other things, besides your Higher Self, are trying to influence you. If you are not fulfilled or happy with the direction of your life, you may be listening to the wrong voice. Let's see what some of the other voices might be. Then you will learn how to tell the difference between those voices and the voice of your true guidance.

If you are not fulfilled or happy with the direction of your life, you may be listening to the wrong voice.

Ego

When people are out of touch with their souls, they tend to rely on the ego for direction. The ego's function is to help us use our gifts and abilities to live the best life we can. The ego tends to be good at getting things done. It wants us to be safe, have whatever we need to live, and feel good about ourselves. This happens automatically when the ego follows the soul's leading, according to its divine plan. It takes more effort, and becomes more stressful, when the ego is out of touch with the soul. The ego then tries to accomplish these goals on its own, setting its own agenda. The ego's agenda may not be in alignment with the divine plan for the individual's life. It may be narrowly focused, difficult to achieve, and ultimately dissatisfying.

The ego may decide, for example, that a certain job or title would provide the income, social status, and lifestyle needed to help an individual feel safe, live better, and improve his or her self esteem. The individual might work day and night to get a particular job. He or she might decide there is no time for self-nurturing, outings with the family, or hobbies. The ego's agenda becomes all-encompassing, putting stress on the individual and his or her family. Joy is driven away by the ego's lack of attention to the individual's needs, its constant demands for perfection, and its narrow focus on the goal. In the end, the individual may or may not get the job. In the meantime, he or she has given up a great deal for something that may not even be necessary.

When the soul and Higher Self lead the way, *all* of the needs of the individual are taken into consideration. The process takes precedence over the goal. There is joy and satisfaction in daily life because the individual is living in alignment with the passions of the soul. There is time for all of the things that are important to the individual—free time, family, hobbies, etc.—because they *are* the stuff of life. The Higher Self sees the bigger picture, and uses synchronicity to make things happen more easily, and in less time. The individual's needs are met, so he or she feels safe, nurtured, and taken care of. The individual also feels good about himself or herself because true self-esteem comes from the soul. It is achieved by living in accordance with one's truth and divine plan. The soul and Higher Self can utilize any number of means to provide the individual and his or her family with whatever they need to live an abundant life.

When the soul and Higher Self lead the way, *all* of the needs of the individual are taken into consideration.

The ego's agenda can sometimes limit the soul's flexibility, mobility, and ability to create the situations that would best accomplish the soul's purposes. The ego's agenda is often based upon the mass consciousness belief systems and fears. It sets goals based on how we think life "should look" rather than what the soul wants to experience. For example, a person who is being guided to change careers may choose not to do so if it would mean a loss of income and change in life style (agendas of the ego). From the perspective of the Higher Self, however, the change might help the individual to better exercise his or her innate gifts and truth. At the same time, new people and circumstances could be drawn into his or her life that would contribute to the lessons, healing, and experiences for which the soul is here (the soul's agenda).

Does this sound familiar? Have you ever been afraid to listen to and follow your inner guidance? Maybe you thought it was too risky. Maybe you were afraid of making a mistake that would be potentially harmful to you, your family, or others. The Higher Self and ego can have very different standards upon which to base their decisions. The ego's voice and commands tend to come from a place of survival, fear, and pride. It does its best to steer clear of the things we fear. The Higher Self supports our best and highest good. It may lead us directly into our fears to help us heal them.

Group Mind

Sometimes the internal voices we hear are those of the various groups to which we belong. They may be the voices of our family, our employers, our religious organizations, the regions in which we live, or various other associations. There is a tendency to want to "fit in", and be an accepted part of, the social structures that make up our lives. This is especially true if those structures are founded on the paradigm of separation, rather than compassion. In the paradigm of

Sometimes the internal voices we hear are those of the various groups to which we belong.

separation, people are made to feel closer by setting themselves apart from others. There is a "we versus they" mentality. It comes through in statements like:

- "We are better than they."
- "We do it right."
- "Our way is the only way to true happiness (salvation, peace, fulfillment, enlightenment, etc.)."

The paradigm of compassion is quite different. Everyone is seen as part of the whole. People's differences are honored and embraced. People seek out others who can add new perspectives, abilities, and ways of doing things. They are drawn together to help round out the whole. Compassion is evident in statements like:

- "We are all equal."
- "All paths serve a purpose."
- "There are many paths to happiness (peace, fulfillment, enlightenment, etc.)."

Many people struggle between following the rules of the group, versus what works for them as individuals. It is easy to feel like an outsider when one goes against the grain of the group. The feeling of being an outsider is a sign that there may be a different and more appropriate path to follow individually. It is tempting to want to follow the group in order to feel part of it. This may not be the path of greatest joy and personal fulfillment.

Let me give you some examples. Some employers expect their employees to devote their lives to the corporation—to be at their beck and call and to work day and night. An internal conflict may develop when an individual wants to spend more time with the family, or do more things of a personal nature. The "corporate voice" can be very strong and alluring. Those that follow the decrees of the company to work overtime might feel like the inner circle. But they may find little joy or satisfaction in the day-to-day grind.

Some families set expectations in terms of education, income, religious affiliation, standards of behavior, or proper selection of a mate for the family members. It is tempting to want to follow these to please the family, and to fit in. But what happens when a family member falls in love with someone not deemed "appropriate"? What if a son finds that higher education is not for him? What if a daughter no longer resonates with the family religion? In the paradigm of separation, sometimes a choice must be made between fitting in with the family and following one's bliss. In the paradigm of compassion, the individual is encouraged to follow the passions of the soul. It does not detract from the cohesiveness of the group.

There are some religious organizations and religious leaders that operate from the paradigm of separation. They insist that their beliefs and traditions are the real true beliefs and proper traditions. Their rules are the ones necessary to follow for attainment of eternal life, salvation, or enlightenment. Those who don't believe or act as they do are not "saved". Splits within the organization occur when a portion of the membership disagrees with the rules or beliefs. Rather than integrating people's differences, they separate into even more narrow factions. People end up leaving the organization because their beliefs don't exactly match up with those of the head governing body.

Organizations that operate from the paradigm of compassion encourage internal searching and questioning of its members. I predict that the most successful spiritual organizations of the future will be those that set very few rules and beliefs for their members. Instead, they will provide the space for non-judgmental dialog of people's ideas. They will help their members to get in touch with their inner selves. They will encourage and support them to find their own path to spiritual fulfillment.

It is very easy to give the reigns of our lives over to another individual or group. It can happen so subversively, that we are not even aware of it. When we are out of touch with the guidance of our own Higher Self, it is tempting to rely on the direction given by another. There is a belief system deeply ingrained in many people that "other people know more than I do". This is one reason why people so readily give up their sovereignty to another. Many people rely on the direction of their religious leaders, or certain angels, saints, or psychics to guide them through life. If one is to truly fulfill the divine plan for his or her life, it is important to maintain contact with the guidance of one's Higher Self, rather than depending on the direction of someone outside oneself.

There is a belief system deeply ingrained in many people that "other people know more than I do".

Sexual Partners

Have you noticed that sometimes the wants, needs, and goals of someone you are very close to become your own wants, needs, and goals? This frequently happens between sexual partners. The sexual connection between people is a soul connection. The energies of the two souls can become intertwined. There can be an overlap of the "radio signal" so that the voice of the other person's Higher Self seems to be the voice of one's own Higher Self. It is a similar connection to that of guru and student, if the guru has a controlling nature and the student has a submissive nature. We may not be consciously aware of the intertwining of souls. But if there is something that doesn't feel right about the goals in your life, or if they are not giving you joy, this can be one area in which to look.

When someone tells us to take a certain direction or make a particular decision, we should always double check with our Higher Selves to see if it is right for us. This includes parents, partners, psychics, religious leaders, or organizations to which we belong. They can give us recommendations, or tell us what they are seeing for our lives. But it is up to us, and no one else, to determine what direction to take. Sometimes we need to consciously release our attachments to other people in order to regain our personal sovereignty. The following exercise will help you to clear your field of some of these attachments, confusing signals, and voices.

Exercise – Clearing Your Field

1. *Ground yourself to the earth and your Higher Self.*
2. *Ask your Higher Self to assist you in clearing your field of voices and energies that no longer serve your highest good and are not in alignment with your soul, Higher Self, and the divine plan for your life.*
3. *Say to yourself, "I break all contracts and agreements, and release all karma, with individuals and entities that no longer serve my highest good or support the divine plan for my life."*
4. *Visualize the cords of attachment (energetic connections) with these individuals dissolving and dissipating.*
5. *Bring in the vibration of forgiveness to heal the wounds and places of attachment.*
6. *Ask your Higher Self if there are any beliefs and behaviors that need to be revised. If so, write them down, along with the new ones that are replacing them.*
7. *Intend that the new beliefs and behaviors be installed, all the way down to your DNA.*
8. *Surround yourself with a protective shield of golden light. You can even add some red rage energy to the shield to help set your boundaries.*

We have seen that there can be many voices that try to influence the direction of our lives. The exercise you just completed can help to reduce the influence of those voices. It is a process, however, and can take some time. The voices tend to return until we have dealt with our fears and issues and balanced our energy. You can go through the exercise whenever that happens.

How do we know when other voices are trying to influence us? How can each of us differentiate between those voices and that of the Higher Self? How do we *know* what is true guidance and what is not?

Guidance or Fantasy?

For our purposes, I will use the word "fantasy" for messages that are not from the Higher Self. This includes anything that is not in alignment with the divine plan for the individual soul. One person's guidance can be another person's fantasy, since the paths and purposes of individuals can be so different.

Fantasies play on our minds, our belief systems, our fears, and our egos to create a life that may look good on the outside, but not necessarily feel right on the inside. That is one reason why there are many successful people, living the "good life", who feel unhappy, empty, or unfulfilled. They are living a life of fantasy, as far as the soul is concerned.

The soul's agenda is the only path that will truly fulfill us. But how do we know whether we are on that path? How can we be sure that the guidance we are receiving is congruent with the soul's agenda? It is not always easy to know whether we are being led by our Higher Selves or being sidetracked by some fantasy. This is actually the most important skill to develop if our intention is to live by our guidance. No matter what methods we use to access our guidance, it is critical to test that guidance to make sure it is in resonance with the Higher Self.

Our *feelings* are the key to discerning whether the messages we are receiving are from the Higher Self and are in alignment with the soul's purposes, or whether they are other voices and fantasies. People have difficulty discerning what is true guidance when they are out of touch with their feelings. Some don't allow themselves to feel their feelings. Others, even when they do feel them, may not really listen to them. It is important to take the time to find out what our feelings are trying to tell us.

Our *feelings* are the key to discerning whether the messages we are receiving are from the Higher Self and are in alignment with the soul's purposes, or whether they are other voices and fantasies.

A major part of tuning into our guidance—our personal signal—is to consciously tune into our feelings. The following are feelings that I have learned to look for when accessing my guidance. These feelings indicate to me whether I am accessing my guidance or creating a fantasy. You may have others.

Heart

When facing a decision, people often tell us, "Follow your heart". This is good advice. True guidance is felt in the heart, because the heart is governed by the Higher Self. The heart chakra allows into it only the energies and messages that resonate with the Higher Self. The rest "bounce off". If the message is in resonance with the Higher Self, an expansion, swelling, opening, or softness is felt in the area of the heart. There is a deep-down feeling that "this is right for me".

If the message causes activity or commotion in the head rather than a welling in the heart, then it is probably a fantasy.

Fantasies are usually felt in the head, and often get stuck there. Here is why:

When we have fears and defense mechanisms, the heart chakra becomes constricted. When constricted, it holds a very limited space just around the heart. The messages that come in through the crown chakra and which do not resonate with the Higher Self bounce off the heart chakra back up into the head and throat. They have no place else to go, so they keep repeating themselves, like an endless tape. Fantasies can become obsessions. All this activity in the head can result in headaches, sleepless nights, and sore necks.

One way to prevent fantasies from taking over is to expand the heart chakra beyond the crown chakra. The expanded heart chakra keeps the nonresonant energies from entering the head in the first place. This makes it much easier to receive clear guidance from the Higher Self. The information and exercises found in Portal #4 are helpful tools for expanding the heart chakra.

One way to prevent fantasies from taking over is to expand the heart chakra beyond the crown chakra.

Connecting the heart and crown chakras prior to seeking guidance is another way to reduce the inaccuracies and distortions of the messages that we receive through the crown chakra. The soul, which is subject to distortion, governs the crown chakra. But it is also our link to our Higher Self. You can connect the heart and crown chakras by calling on your soul and Higher Self to unite in your heart and collaborate for your highest good, prior to seeking guidance.

Peace and Calm

Guidance is delivered with peace and calm. There is a feeling of steadiness. The energy is smooth and even feeling. It is felt as a very grounded, quiet, presence—the "still small voice" that arises from the core of one's being.

Fantasy, on the other hand, has a feeling of excitement. We have come to believe that excitement is a great thing—the spice of life. But it can be very misleading if we think that it comes from the Higher Self. It is usually a product of the ego and mind, and causes a good deal of surface turbulence. Fantasies are frequently accompanied by an emotional charge that can range from feeling high and on top of the world to feeling anxious or depressed. These ungrounded feelings are quite different from the grounded, centered, peaceful feeling associated with true guidance.

Passion

Passion comes from the soul. Guidance is therefore often accompanied by a feeling of deep passion, as if one were dipping into a very deep well. There is a "clunked-in" feeling that the round peg has found its round hole. One must be careful not to mistake excitement for passion. Excitement is a surface energy. Passion is much deeper.

Fantasies frequently proceed from feelings of expectation, obligation, guilt, or duty. Sometimes the expectations come from others, and sometimes they are our own. Should's, must-do's, fearful thoughts, and guilt do not play a part in true guidance. There is no passion in that. It is advisable to reconsider one's decisions if they are being made out of obligation or guilt. True guidance will not lead one to do something that is against one's nature. Fantasies, on the other hand, may do just that.

Should's, must-do's, fear, and guilt do not play a part in true guidance. There is no passion in that.

Joy

Because true guidance is in alignment with the soul's purpose, there is an inherent joy that comes from following it. Some people call this "following your bliss". It feels like the soul is dancing. Guidance brings joy into the present moment. It does not make promises of a future time when all will be well, although that is oftentimes the outcome. Instead, it guides one into being in joy *now,* based on one's state of "being" as the guidance is followed.

> Guidance brings joy into the present moment.

For example, Eric has fantasized that if he works harder than most, he will land a high-paying job that will help him send his children to college. Eric is having an internal conflict between spending more time at work and spending time with his family. Guidance may very well tell him to take the time for family. This will increase his joy *now.* If college is part of the divine plan for his children's lives, it will be provided for without Eric having to miss out on their growing-up years.

Fantasies are more *future* and *"doing"* oriented. Fantasies frequently ask one to endure the suffering of the present moment in order to accomplish a future goal. They tend to be an escape into "happiness" that masks the pain, fear, or suffering that one is currently experiencing. In Eric's case, his fantasy of having a good-paying job requires that he spend more time at work and less time with his family. Eric escapes his present misery by focusing on the rosy future that lies ahead. There is some excitement in it, but little joy.

Trust

True guidance is based on trust. A vision may be given with little awareness of how it will manifest, as was the case with the truck driver. Guidance is usually given one step at a time on an as-needed basis as close to the present time as possible.

This not only prevents the mind from interfering, but also allows the Higher Self much more flexibility in creating synchronicities as circumstances change.

> Guidance is usually given one step at a time on an as-needed basis as close to the present time as possible.

Fantasies, on the other hand, oftentimes are long-range plans for the future. The ego uses the mind to create a linear, step-by-step process to achieve its goals. It tries to tie things together into neat little packages. This leaves very little room for spontaneity and flexibility—two essential ingredients of following one's guidance.

The ego may not understand the logic behind the direction of the Higher Self. It might say, "This doesn't make sense" or "I don't know how this can possibly be done" or "I might suffer if I do this". It creates fantasies to make us feel safe. It is very easy to get caught up in fears of not being taken care of, not having a bankroll, not having retirement reserves, etc. If this is our focus, then that is what we will experience.

When these fears come up, it is an opportunity to heal them. We don't want to submerge them or ignore them. We want to go into them to balance and integrate them, as you learned how to do in Portal #4. Then we are able to live by our guidance moment by moment to allow our lives to unfold gracefully, easily, and abundantly, without fear.

It may feel like a risk to follow one's guidance, but the opposite is actually true. The risk comes from *not* following our guidance. When we follow our guidance, the abundance of the Universe comes forth in unexpected ways. The more you follow your guidance, the more you will trust its wisdom.

> It may feel like a risk to follow one's guidance, but the opposite is actually true.

Satisfaction

Following one's guidance brings a feeling of present moment satisfaction. When being guided step by step in the present moment, it is the process that becomes important. Life becomes very satisfying because it is really lived in the here and now, and is in alignment with the soul's purpose.

With fantasy there is a feeling of longing or striving. The goal or outcome takes precedence, and the present moment is forgotten. Some people get so caught up in carrying out their fantasies that they put off living their lives. Young people may miss out on their youth because they can't wait to fall in love, get married, own a home, have children, etc. Career people may miss out on the satisfactions of their present job as they long for a bigger office, a fancier title, or the next promotion.

Fantasies can be very alluring. They are usually exciting and make us feel good about ourselves. For a time, they may give us something to work for, provide an illusion of security, and help us to "fit in" with society. But in the end, they are not satisfying.

Think about how many times you or someone you knew felt the temporary "high" of attaining a goal, only to be back in the doldrums days or weeks later, looking for the next big mountain to climb. Unless we are aware of the subtle differences in how fantasies and true guidance feel, it is easy to get caught up in the whirlwind life of fantasy, never finding the true, deep, satisfaction that comes from fulfilling the soul's purposes on earth.

Nonattachment

True guidance is not attached to results or a particular outcome. Life is allowed to flow with the guidance received. That does not mean that there are no results. There certainly are. But they may or may not be the ones that we think will occur.

It is very tempting to attach an outcome to a piece of information that is received. However, the outcomes that the mind creates may have little or nothing to do with the guidance given. For example, about the time I left my engineering job, I was guided to write a book on relationships. I was given the title and outline for the book, and a good deal of information on what to include. I spent about a year working on that book—developing a thorough outline as information came through to me, writing a book proposal, and submitting it to publishers and agents. In the process, my relationships with others grew, evolved, and healed as I used the information in my personal life.

Then I was guided to tuck the proposal away and go to massage school. That particular book is still waiting to be written. Perhaps it will never be written. But the information that was given to me has been invaluable in my own personal relationships. Guidance never promised me that the book would be published—only that I should work on it.

Had I been attached to getting that book written and published, perhaps I would have delayed becoming a massage therapist and developing my awareness of the body. Perhaps I would have been too "busy" to devote time to other aspects of my own inner healing, which resulted in the writing of *this* book. Guidance has its own timing and purpose for everything. Sometimes we simply never will know *why* we were led to do a particular thing. Thinking that every path is perfectly straight, or leads directly to a "finish line", is a fantasy that can sidetrack us. Part of the lesson in learning to listen to and follow our guidance is to allow the Higher Self to set the course, no matter how disjointed it may look from this earthly perspective.

Thinking that every path is perfectly straight, or leads directly to a "finish line", is a fantasy that can sidetrack us.

Freedom

True guidance supports the path of freedom and self-expression. There is a feeling of being set free when we follow our guidance, because we are honoring the true expression of our soul. A "free spirit" is a joyful spirit. Life becomes more spontaneous as we let go of the reins and follow our guidance moment by moment, allowing life to unfold freely.

Fantasies are commonly based on ideas, beliefs, and obsessions that control us and therefore limit our freedom. We can have obsessions with a particular person, place, idea, or thing—with something we must do or someone we *must* have so as to feel complete, safe, or happy. Rather than being grounded in love, fantasies are held in place by illusion and fear of loss. The things in our lives that somehow control us also constrict our energy, prevent us from following our true path, and limit the freedom of others and ourselves.

Ease

Since guidance comes moment by moment, there is no need for stress regarding what is going to happen next year, next week, or even the next day. The focus is on the task at hand because the plan is allowed to evolve over time. This is calming and energizing. There is a sense of ease. It may seem as if time is being used inefficiently. But the soul has its own reasons for having us do things in a particular order. Many synchronicities happen when this is allowed, and things actually happen with much more ease than when everything is planned out in advance.

Fantasies are contrived. Because there is usually an anticipated goal or result, tremendous energy is expended in planning for and trying to achieve the goal and result within a certain time frame. Adrenaline is released causing tension that may temporarily feel like a spike in energy. But all the planning, thinking, and adrenaline rushes eventually cause stress and fatigue. In addition to that, there is a feeling of wading through quicksand as goals that are not in alignment with the divine plan for one's life become difficult to achieve.

We have discussed many things that differentiate true guidance from fantasy. Below is a summary of the feelings, thoughts, and qualities that are indicative of true guidance versus those that come from fantasy. It may be used to help you discern whether the messages you are receiving are true guidance or not.

The Difference Between Guidance and Fantasy

GUIDANCE	FANTASY
Felt in the heart	Felt in the head
Expansive	Limited
Calm and peaceful	Exciting and turbulent
Still small voice	Noisy thoughts
Grounded	Out of body
Follows one's passion	Done out of expectation
Aligned with soul's essence	Against one's nature
Inherently joyful	Escape into happiness
"Being" oriented	"Doing" oriented
Based on trust	Rooted in fear, worry, lack
Creative and nonlinear	Logical and linear
Given one step at a time	Wants all the answers now
Flexible	Set in stone
Moment to moment	Future oriented
Spontaneous	Planned
Present moment satisfaction	Longing and striving
Process based	Goal based
Not attached to results	Requires results
Feeling of freedom	Feeling of control
Letting go	Obsessive
Allowed to unfold	Contrived
Makes life easier	Produces stress
Evolving	Absolute

Not all of the qualities listed need to be present simultaneously. Most of the time they will present themselves in various combinations, depending on the content and purpose of the guidance or fantasy. It is also possible to have a medley of feelings that represent both guidance and fantasy at the same time. This happens when guidance is given on something, and then the ego and mind create a fantasy around it. As an example, let's take Laura's situation—a fairly common one.

Laura has recently received guidance that a change of jobs is to occur. This is true guidance, so Laura is feeling joyful and peaceful about it. At the same time, Laura's ego kicks into gear and begins to ask questions like, "When will this happen; what job am I to take; and what will be my position and income?" The ego's job is to get things done. So it is anxious to begin looking for another job.

Laura's mind begins to create its own version of her ideal job. It tells her that the job should be close to home, pay well, and utilize her skills. It urges her to apply to the Nirvana Company, since it is close to home. Laura becomes excited over the prospect of a shorter commute. But she also fears that no one will hire her, and worries about how well Nirvana Co. will pay.

Laura's mind is already in full gear, fantasizing over the outcome of the guidance she has received. So far, Laura's guidance has told her nothing about the specifics of the job change. All she really knows is that, sometime in the future, she will have a change of jobs. She is at peace with that. But because her mind and ego are trying to seize control of the situation, she is beginning to stress over the specifics of it. The feeling of peace comes from hearing her guidance. The excitement, stress, and worry are products of her fantasies.

This is an example of how feelings of true guidance and feelings of fantasy can be present at the same time. It is a frequent occurrence. The way around it is to allow our guidance to lead us every step of the way, and not allow the mind and ego to take a small tidbit of information and run away with it. To do this takes patience, and the ability to wait. I once waited more than a year between the time I received the guidance that I would have a career change and the time that it actually happened. But when it finally did happen, everything just fell into place with ease.

The ego tends to want to take control out of fear, guilt, or pride. If we detect that any of these are influencing our decisions, it is wise to ask the Higher Self what it truly desires. It may give us a different answer or path to consider that would be more in alignment with the divine plan for our lives. Or it may tell us that no action at the moment is the best course to take.

The ego tends to want to take control out of fear, guilt, or pride.

In the example above, sorting through her feelings will help Laura to determine what is guidance and what is fantasy so that her job change will happen in the proper timing and sequence, and the right job will be found. Being attentive to our feelings and following the guidance of our Higher Selves every step of the way is the key to living the divine plan for our lives with ease and not going off on tangents of the mind and ego.

Being attentive to our feelings and following the guidance of our Higher Selves every step of the way is the key to living the divine plan for our lives with ease and not going off on tangents of the mind and ego.

The exercise on the following page is designed to help you tell the difference between true guidance and fantasy through your feelings.

Exercise – Listening to Your Feelings

1. *Consider a question that you currently have about your life. It might be something like, "Am I to stay in my present job (home, relationship, etc.) at this time?"; "Am I supposed to go to college next year?"; or "Am I to take a trip to Spain this Fall?".*

2. *Write down the various options that you are considering. "Yes, I am supposed to attend college next year" or "No, I am not supposed to attend college next year". Do not combine too many variables. (Which college to attend, should the answer be yes, is another question and set of alternatives).*

3. *Consider each alternative one by one. Take your time. What feelings arise for you as you consider the alternative? Look at the list provided previously to determine whether these feelings are coming from guidance or fantasy. For example, when you think about going to college, do you feel a sense of peace, calm, and steadiness in your heart (an indication that guidance is at work) or do you feel pressure in your head, excitement, and turbulence? Are you feeling that you SHOULD go to college rather than KNOWING that college is for you? These are signs that the mind and ego have created a fantasy.*

4. *Do you have both a peaceful feeling in your heart and a head full of concerns and questions? Do fears surface surrounding the issue? Trust the path that is giving you peace and allow your Higher Self to work with you on the details that are giving you concern. Practice surrender, as you were shown how to do in Portal #4.*

Fear

There are certain times when a feeling of fear *is* guidance. It is different from the fears that torture the mind and come from the ego. It is more of a body awareness, like a sixth sense, that something is wrong. The source of the fear may be unknown. Sometimes people get this feeling when a person they are close to is in trouble, even though they have no conscious awareness of it. Other times the feeling arises when a person is about to do something that may be harmful to him or her. I had such a feeling in August of 2001.

I was on the Internet making flight reservations for a trip to New York City to hear my friend Jane speak at the United Nations. We were also going to get together to discuss a project that we were planning to create together.

My scheduled departure date was September 11, 2001. I have flown often, and am not afraid to fly, so I was very surprised when I started to get a sick, gnawing feeling in my stomach when the early morning flight times came up on the screen. It worsened when I saw that I was to transfer through Washington, D.C. I thought perhaps I was balking over spending the money, and ran forgiveness and surrender through the fear of not having enough. It didn't help.

The anxious feeling persisted. I had no idea why I felt that way, so I decided to hold off making my reservations. The next day Jane sent me an e-mail to let me know that we would not be able to spend much time together discussing the project. She needed the time to prepare for her talk. That did it. I decided to cancel my plans. Perhaps I was supposed to be doing something else that week.

Jane was feeling a bit abandoned because, one by one, people who had said they would attend her talk cancelled their plans and plane reservations. Another mutual friend of ours, who hadn't planned on going, stepped up to the plate and said, "I'll go!" But the next day her guidance told her in no uncertain terms to stay home.

The morning of September 11, 2001, the sick feeling in my stomach returned when I heard the news of the airliners crashing into the World Trade Center towers in New York City and into the Pentagon in Washington, D.C. A short time later, I recalled that that was the exact morning I was supposed to have flown to New York, through Washington. I thanked my Higher Self for sparing me the trauma of that trip. As it turned out, I met with various local friends, spending the time in meditation with them and sending light to the souls in transition. My Higher Self did indeed have other plans for the use of my time and energy that day.

Guidance comes to us in so many ways. Our feelings are important indicators of what is true and what is fantasy. They should always be consulted when considering information of any kind.

Ways of Receiving Guidance

We have spoken at length about the inner voices and urgings that can guide us. Let us address some of the other ways we receive guidance. Many people believe that guidance is something to search for and find outside of themselves. They think that divine revelation must come from a source such as an angel, saint, deceased relative, spirit guide, or guru. They look to another being (physical or non-physical) to provide wisdom and direction for their lives. Sometimes this is done through means such as prayer, meditation, shamanic journeying, or psychic readings. These methods can be effective and very helpful. But we must *always* double check with our feelings to make sure that the information from outside sources resonates with the Higher Self.

We must *always* double check with our feelings to make sure that the information from outside sources resonates with the Higher Self.

We do have the capability of intuiting our own guidance. In fact, whether we are aware of it or not, most of the time we are doing exactly that. Many of the methods for increasing one's psychic and intuitive abilities are discussed in a wonderful book called *The Psychic Pathway*[1], by Sonia Choquette, Ph.D. Dr. Choquette is a gifted psychic and healer who has helped thousands of people get in touch with their inner selves through her books, seminars, and personal healing work. I highly recommend her book if you are feeling stuck in this area, or simply wish to increase your intuitive ability.

People have their own preferred ways of accessing their guidance. I will give you a few of mine. You might want to experiment to see which ones work best for you.

Inspirational Writing

Inspirational writing is done by first asking a question, and then recording whatever comes to mind. It is not composed. It just flows. The process of writing helps to direct and focus one's thoughts, providing clarity to the jumble of thoughts that are floating around in one's head. It is similar to the process that Neale Donald Walsch used while writing his series of books entitled *Conversations With God*[2].

Sometimes what is written may not seem to make sense at the time. When the answer is read, however, additional thoughts that expand and clarify what has been recorded may come to mind. I frequently use inspirational writing when I journal. I receive guidance on questions that come up in the course of my daily life. It is interesting to reread the daily entries a year or two later and see how all the pieces of information fit together. I have found it reaffirming. It has

---

[1] Sonia Choquette, Ph.D., *The Psychic Pathway (A Workbook for Reawakening the Voice of Your Soul)*, New York: Three Rivers Press, 1995.

[2] Neale Donald Walsch, *Conversations With God, Book 1: an uncommon dialogue*, New York: Putnam Pub Group, 1996.

deepened my level of trust in my guidance. You may wish to use the protocol below when using inspirational writing to access your guidance.

Exercise – Inspirational Writing

1. *Ground yourself to the earth and your Higher Self.*
2. *Center yourself, calling upon your Higher Self to expand your heart chakra beyond your crown chakra.*
3. *Ask that the Higher Self join with the soul in the heart to give you answers that are in alignment with the divine plan for your life, and that are for your best and highest good.*
4. *Write down the question.*
5. *Record the answer without thinking about it.*
6. *Read the answer and write down any further information that comes through.*
7. *Test the validity of the information using the exercise on listening to your feelings given on* *page 260.*

Meditation

When the mind is focused, it is much easier for the soul and Higher Self to use it as a receptor of information. Meditation trains the mind to stay focused. Once the mind is calm, clear, and focused, a process similar to inspirational writing may be used to receive guidance. After the question is asked, the answer may come as a word, statement, vision, or feeling. The answer may then be validated by consulting one's feelings. It is not necessary to write down the answer, but I often do just to have a record of it.

Conversation

Conversation is another way of focusing the mind. Simply bouncing our ideas off another person can give clarity to our thoughts. Sometimes, when I am in conversation with another, my questions will be answered through something that one of us says. Many times they are inspired—ideas that neither of us have thought of previously, but that just flow spontaneously out of our mouths. People can act as antennas for one another in this regard. Just make sure that the answer you receive is for *you*, and not the other person. Test it with your feelings.

Dreams

Guidance may come in a dream. Our souls do an amazing amount of work while we sleep. Before retiring, ground yourself and ask your Higher Self to give you guidance through your dreams. You can ask a specific question, or leave it open-ended. Keep paper and pencil by your bed to record your dreams when you wake up. You can use inspirational writing or meditation to help you interpret your dreams, or you can use dream analysis. A book I found to be very helpful for interpreting dreams is *Inner Work*[3] by Robert A. Johnson.

Spontaneous Promptings

In my experience, most of the time guidance happens spontaneously. I will get the urge to call someone, and find out she needed to talk to a friend that day. I will see someone in emotional turmoil, and be moved to offer assistance on the spot. I will get the feeling that today I should do some cleaning and, soon after, unexpected company arrives. Even the vision for this whole series of books came to me one morning while I was brushing my teeth! Guidance can and should be a natural part of our lives, in things both big and small. An essential ingredient for making

> Guidance can and should be a natural part of our lives, in things both big and small.

[3] Robert A. Johnson, *Inner Work (Using Dreams & Active Imagination for Personal Growth)*, San Francisco: Harper 1986.

> An essential ingredient for making our guidance a natural part of our lives is to stay centered in the present moment.

our guidance a natural part of our lives is to stay centered in the present moment. The here and now is where the soul resides. That is where it speaks to us. It is also where we are most aware and sensitive.

It becomes relatively straightforward to follow the leading of the Higher Self moment by moment when we can tell the difference between guidance and fantasy. It does take some practice, however. Until we become accustomed to how guidance from the Higher Self feels, it may be wise to double-check it using an additional method. Kinesiology and dowsing are two techniques that have worked for me.

Kinesiology

The body has direct access to the soul's vibrations. This is called "Body Knowing". I experienced a form of body knowing when I was guided to cancel my reservations to New York. The body can be used to gain answers to our many questions. One way is through our feelings, as we have already discussed. Another way is through muscle testing, also known as *Kinesiology*.

Muscle testing is based on the precept that our muscles are stronger when exposed to things that are good for us and that are in alignment with the soul. Correspondingly, the muscles weaken when subjected to something that is not in alignment with, or resonant with, the body or soul. These can include things like thoughts, energies, activities, circumstances, or foods. Because of this, Kinesiology can be used to determine allergies to certain foods. The muscles weaken when foods to which it is allergic are placed in the mouth. The same thing can happen simply by thinking about those foods, and asking about their effects on the body. The muscles weaken when asked about foods that are detrimental, and strengthen when asked about foods that are nutritious and beneficial.

Likewise, when the body is asked about various directions for one's life, the muscles strengthen when the direction is in alignment with the soul, and weaken when it is not. The answers to all kinds of questions can be obtained through muscle testing. We can ask questions about such matters as relationships, living arrangements, jobs, diet, unconscious issues and fears we might have, trips we are planning to take, the underlying causes of a particular ailment, or how to spend our time and money.

The answers to all kinds of questions can be obtained through muscle testing.

Muscle testing can also be used to get answers for other people *if we have their permission to do so,* either in person or from their Higher Selves. If you are asking the person's Higher Self for permission, muscle test whether you have it. If you do, ask the question and muscle test for the answer. If you don't have permission, it is best to leave it alone. Sometimes I will consult another's Higher Self in how to best assist that person. For example, if Marty is having physical problems, I might ask his Higher Self if I should send him light, offer to do an intuitive session, help him clean his house, or do nothing.

When muscle testing, the phrasing of the questions is of key importance. They must be questions with "yes" or "no" answers. They should be as clear and unambiguous as possible. The same question can have two entirely different answers if a clarification is added to it.

For example, if I ask whether I am to take a trip to Chicago, I might get a yes. If I ask whether I am to go to Chicago next week, I might get a no. The first question implies that a trip to Chicago will be made sometime in the future. The second question asks whether it is to be done at a particular time. Of course, one can start with a general question and then narrow it down. A "yes" to the question "Am I to go to Chicago?" can be narrowed down to a specific time frame with further questioning. The chart contains some examples of questions that are clear and specific, and those that are open ended and ambiguous.

Composing Clear Questions

Clear "Yes and No" Questions	**Ambiguous Questions (needs further clarification)**
Is my name Amber?	What is my name? (not a yes or no question)
Is it for my best and highest good to end my cleansing fast today?	Should I end my cleansing fast? (when?)
Is it for my best and highest good to change jobs within the next year? (You can narrow this down further—next six months, next week, etc.)	Will I be changing jobs? (when?)
Is it within the divine plan for my life to partner with David at this time?	Will David be my life partner? (beginning now, or when?)

Practice by asking questions to which you know the answers. This will help you to learn how to phrase your questions so that they represent your intentions and result in precise answers. Besides the phrasing of the questions, there are several other factors that determine the validity of the answers we receive. They are discussed below.

Hydration

A high proportion of the body's weight is water. Good hydration increases the body's ability to give accurate answers. You may be dehydrated and not even know it. Pinch the skin on the back of your hand. If it does not go right back into place, you are probably dehydrated. Drinking a glass of water prior to muscle testing is a good practice to follow.

Grounding

The soul must be grounded in the body in order for the body to accurately represent the soul. If it is not grounded, the answers may be opposite of the true representation of the soul. One way to test whether you are getting accurate answers is to ask the question, "Is my name __________ (insert your correct first name)?" If the answer is "no" to your correct name, a reverse polarization has probably occurred, causing the soul to be ungrounded.

The soul must be grounded in the body in order for the body to accurately represent the soul.

If being ungrounded is a problem, you may wish to review Portal #1 on grounding to determine the cause. If there is a problem with your etheric gridwork or grounding information, you will find help there. As was mentioned in that chapter, one of the main causes of reverse polarization and ungroundedness is running the energy signature that is opposite to one's gender. Intend that the proper energy signature be run; intend to ground again; and then repeat the question. If grounding continues to be a problem, ask your Higher Self what is causing the problem.

There may be a conflict between the masculine and feminine within or a denial of various aspects of your own gender. In that case, you may wish to do more work on integrating your masculine and feminine sides, as addressed in Portal #6. No matter what the cause, ask whether there is karma involved and for clarification of the thoughts, behaviors, and beliefs associated with it. Intend that it be healed and then run forgiveness through it all.

Fantasy

Sometimes we can get different answers to the same question. In that case, try clarifying the question further. If there is still confusion, there may be an element of fantasy involved. The mind or ego might have one agenda, and the soul another. Or different aspects of the soul may be in conflict, with one aspect unconsciously sabotaging another aspect. Or an outside influence might be adding confusion. In that case, intend that the divine plan for your life be accomplished. Center yourself and expand your heart chakra as much as possible. Also intend to be completely neutral to the answer, so that the mind and ego do not interfere. There are energies available to us that neutralize fantasy. You can ground yourself to the earth and your Higher Self and intend that these energies neutralize any fantasy that might be present.

Timing

There are times when the answers don't come immediately. The ego wants answers and it wants them *now*. The Higher Self does not always work that way. It may know that the timing is not yet right. In that case, the answer will be revealed at a more appropriate time.

At one point I was pressuring myself to decide whether to self-publish this book or to find an established publishing house for it. I asked for guidance on the matter and was told to just "let it go" and focus on my writing.

A couple of months later, synchronicities began to occur. People started showing up to offer assistance should I decide to self-publish. One would do the editing. Another would do the design work. A third would develop the website. A fourth would show me how to market it over the Internet. The money became available. It didn't take long for me to realize that I was being guided to self-publish, and that it would be done with a great deal of help and ease. Had I received that answer two months before, I would have spent needless energy fretting over how I would handle all the details, and how I would pay for it. My Higher Self had compassionately delayed the answer until I could see that I would have the help I needed.

Most of the time, guidance is short-range. It happens close to the time that we are to act on it. This takes a lot of the stress out of life, if we are willing to let go of our need to plan. I have always considered my ability to plan to be one of my strengths. However, as I have grown more and more in touch with my guidance, I have let go of much of my need to plan. I have discovered that my soul and Higher Self work things out synchronistically quite well on their own. If I simply follow their leading step by step, much of the needless footwork is eliminated. Guidance can change from one day to the next due to timing. The following story is a good case in point.

Most of the time, guidance is short-range. It happens close to the time that we are to act on it.

Because of a medical condition, my Father was in need of some added assistance in his home. My brothers and sisters and I agreed to provide this for a couple of months, at which time we would re-evaluate his condition and our abilities to provide it. At the end of the two months, all of us, including Dad, felt it was time to find some outside help. I began to ask people I knew for phone numbers of people who gave in-home assistance. However, my guidance told me it was not yet time to make any phone calls.

The next day, as I walked past a woman at work, I was guided to ask her if she knew of someone. She told me that her daughter was coming home from college and looking for summer employment. We began to discuss the possibility of her helping Dad. We discovered that they lived only two blocks from Dad. This was perfect for her daughter, who didn't have a car to get to work. It was perfect for Dad, too, who needed someone for short periods of time during the day. Not only that, but she had gone through some of the same physical maladies that Dad had, so they had much in common! The ease with which this came about was incredible. It happened because I was willing to be patient and follow the leading of my guidance.

There are other times when a vision is given for our lives that is more long-range, such as that of the truck driver at the beginning of this chapter. These visions prepare us for changes that are coming. The actual accomplishment of the vision may be months or years down the road. In that case, I would advise writing the vision down and asking your Higher Self if there is anything you should do about it now. If there is nothing to do, let it go until you do get some guidance about it. Don't let your ego try to make it happen before its time. If the vision brings up some anxiety, then use the time to heal whatever fears and issues might be surfacing which could prevent you from carrying out the vision.

Divine Plan

Guidance works best when it is supported by the sincere desire to follow the leading of the Higher Self in order to assist the soul for its best and highest good. The Higher Self is not here to meet the demands of the ego. Sometimes we will get answers that seem inaccurate. This is because more accurate answers would not serve the soul's path. Trying to muscle test for the winning lottery number or winner of the Kentucky Derby, for example, may be met with disappointing results, if it is not within the divine plan for the soul's life to experience such things.

There are many ways to muscle test on oneself or on others. Some use the hands or arms; others use the whole body. Below is a step-by-step process for muscle testing on oneself, along with several possible hand and finger configurations. Following that are instructions for using the whole body. You might want to try them all to see what works best for you.

Exercise – General Instructions for Muscle Testing

1. *Ground yourself to the earth and your Higher Self. Run the earth energies up your body (and into your hands for finger testing).*
2. *Expand your heart chakra and set the intention to disconnect from any other source of truth or energy apart from that coming from your own Higher Self—your own guidance.*
3. *Align the soul and Higher Self in the heart.*
4. *Intend neutrality (impartiality) so as not to skew the results.*
5. *Test the accuracy by asking a question to which you know the answer (such as "Is my name...?). Test for a "yes" answer and a "no" answer.*
6. *Carefully phrase the questions you ask. Be clear, concise, and precise. You can use this for guidance on anything from which foods to eat, to what movies to watch, to determining what to do each day.*

Use the above instructions in conjunction with any of the following specific methods of muscle testing.

Muscle Testing Using the Hands

Closed Circle, Thumb, and Index Finger

- *Create a closed circle with the thumb and index finger of your non-dominant hand (ex. left hand).*
- *With your dominant hand (right hand), insert your thumb and index fingers up through the bottom of the circle of your left hand.*
- *After having asked a question, push apart the thumb and index finger of your right hand with the same pressure as that holding the circle together on your left hand. If the circle of your left hand holds firmly together, the answer is YES; if it breaks apart, the answer is NO.*

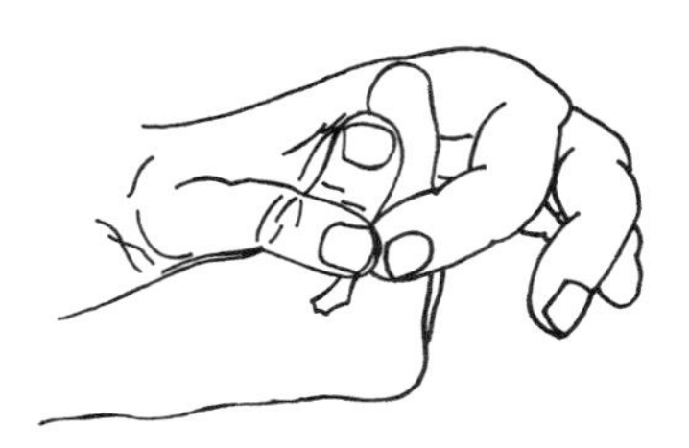

Two Closed Circles

- *Create two closed circles with the thumb and index fingers of both hands, interlocking the circles with each other like a chain.*
- *Ask a question, and then try pulling the circles apart. If the circles will not separate, the answer is YES; if they break apart, the answer is NO.*

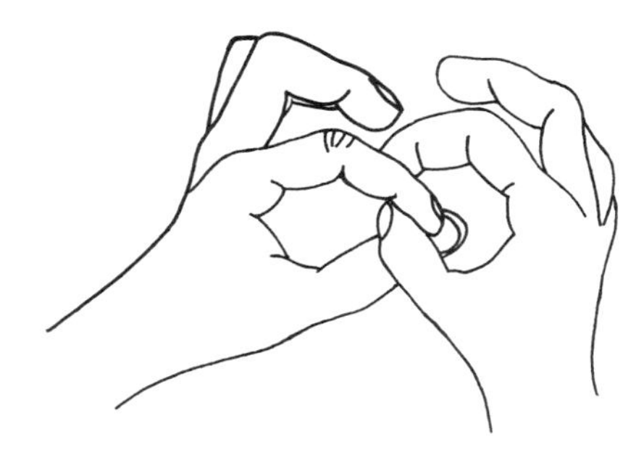

One Closed Circle and One Finger

- *Create a closed circle with the thumb and little finger of your non-dominant hand (ex. left hand).*
- *Insert either the index finger or the little finger of your dominant (right) hand through the circle.*
- *Ask a question and try pushing the finger of your dominant (right) hand through where the thumb and little finger meet of your non-dominant (left) hand. Use equal pressure with both hands. If the circle holds firmly together, the answer is YES; if it breaks apart, the answer is NO.*

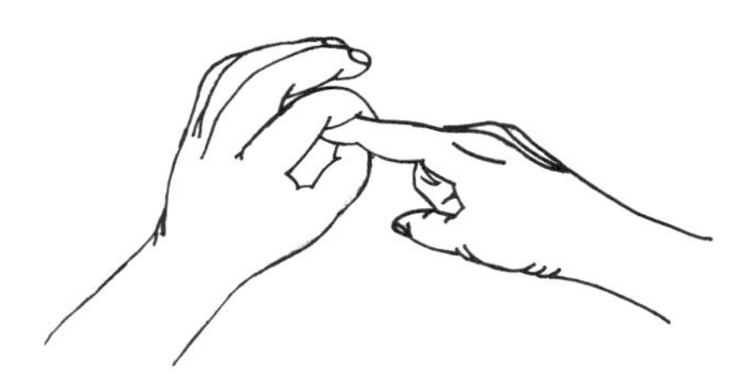

Muscle Testing Using the Whole Body

1. *Stand up.*
2. *Follow the general instructions for muscle testing.*
3. *Write out your question, or take whatever you are testing (food, book, movie, etc.), and place it over the area of your heart.*
4. *Ask a yes or no question—something like, "Is this good for me?" or "Is this for my best and highest good?"*
5. *If your body rocks forward, the answer is YES. If it rocks backward, the answer is NO.*

When muscle testing using the whole body, it is not always necessary to hold an object over the heart. One may simply ask a yes or no question and then observe which way the body rocks.

Dowsing

Another way that guidance can come through the body's energy is through dowsing. Some people prefer this to muscle testing, finding it to be less influenced by the mind. Others prefer muscle testing because it does not require any special equipment, and can be done discreetly. I have found both to be useful.

The six general steps used for muscle testing are also used when dowsing, and the format for asking questions is the same. The most common dowsing tool used to obtain personal guidance is a small pendulum. The direction of its swing determines whether the answer to the question is yes or no. The proper use of a pendulum is beautifully described in the book *The Psychic Pathway*[4], so I will not repeat it here. The American Society of Dowsers, Inc. [5] carries many different pendulums, along with books on the art of dowsing and the use of the pendulum.

Muscle testing and dowsing are tools for accessing one's guidance through body knowing. There are many things that can influence the accuracy of our body knowing through these means, as was mentioned. It is therefore wise to also consult one's feelings. If there seems to be confusion, it is an opportunity to reflect upon what is causing the confusion, work with it, and heal it. You have been given many tools and exercises for healing such things throughout this book.

> Muscle testing and dowsing are tools for accessing one's guidance through body knowing.

---

[4] Sonia Choquette, Ph.D., *The Psychic Pathway (A Workbook for Reawakening the Voice of Your Soul)*, New York: Three Rivers Press, 1995, pp. 230-237.

[5] The American Society of Dowsers, Inc., P.O. Box 24, Danville, VT, 05828-0024; (802) 684-3417; 1-800-711-9497 (bookstore); www.dowsers.org; ASD@dowsers.org.

Knowing how to access our guidance is a very important aspect of soaring with our souls. Guidance helps us to live life with ease; it shows us the path of greatest joy; it helps us to fulfill the divine plan for our lives; and it helps us to live life from the integrity of our souls.

The soul speaks to us in many ways. This book was written to help you get in touch with your soul and Higher Self so that you could know and interpret what your spirit is saying, and heal your life. I hope that it has helped you to become more open and aware of the tremendous wisdom and insight at your disposal right within you.

Each time you re-read a paragraph or chapter of this book, your Higher Self may use it as an opportunity to reveal something new. A change in circumstances a month or year from now could foster entirely different revelations. So feel free to read it again and again, or use it as a basis for your daily quiet time.

There are countless ways to access the soul. This book contains methods that my own Higher Self gave to me, simply by asking. You might want to ask your Higher Self to show you other techniques that are right for you. They may be far different from the methods given here. Be confident that whatever ways you are given are perfect for you.

We are each unique in how we step through these seven portals to mend our lives and discover the wisdom and magnificence of our souls. Tapping into the essence and wisdom of my soul has given me more joy, peace, healing, and love than I ever thought possible on this earth. I hope that it has done, and will continue to do, the same for you.

The Next Level

There is joy; and there is lack of joy. The choice is ours to make. The next book in the *Soaring With Your Soul* series will show you how to take the information provided by your soul and Higher Self to actually live life from your soul. This is the path of greatest joy. It will show you how to know, be, and live the truth of who you are. The impact of this is far-reaching. It is the key to personal fulfillment. It is also the means by which we create true harmony in our interactions with others at all levels—personal, institutional, societal, and global. There is incomparable joy in being who we truly are and living the life we are meant to live. It is the next level of soaring with your soul...

> The path of greatest joy
> is the path of the soul.

You are invited to visit www.bridgesofunity.com for announcements of upcoming books and seminars, free helpful articles, links to other websites, and merchandise created from the heart.

Index

A

B

C

D

E

G

H

I

J

K

L

M

N

O

P

R

S

Do You Know Others Who Would Benefit From Reading This Book?

Use the order form on the reverse side to send your friends and family copies of this book. Sponsor an in-home study group and support one another on your spiritual journey. There is a 20% discount on five or more books.

Bridges of Unity

Bridging Body and Soul

P.O. Box 15727
Loves Park, IL 61132
U.S.A.

www.bridgesofunity.com
orders@bridgesofunity.com
Phone / Fax 1-815-636-2867

Contact the Author

Have you found this book to be helpful? The author would very much like to hear from you. She invites you to write to her at the address above with your stories, comments, and feedback. Or e-mail her at Marcia.Phillips@bridgesofunity.com.

For inquiries on workshops, seminars, or personal intuitive healing sessions, Marcia Phillips invites you to e-mail, fax, call, or visit www.bridgesofunity.com.

Mail Order Form

Mail Order: Please make check payable in US Dollars to:
Bridges of Unity, P.O. Box 15727, Loves Park, IL 61132, U.S.A.

Name: ______________________________

Address: ______________________________

City: ____________________ State: ______________

Postal Code____________________ Country: ____________

Telephone: ______________________________

E-mail Address: ______________________________

Item	Qty	Amount	Price
Seven Portals to Your Soul		$14.95 ea	
Sales Tax (Illinois only)		7.25%	
Shipping & Handling		$ 2.95	
Each additional book		$ 0.95 ea	
Total			

Take 20% discount on 5 or more books

Priority Mail: $5.00 for first book; $2.00 each additional book.

International Airmail: $10.00 for first book; $5.00 each additional book.

Credit Card: Please order through www.bridgesofunity.com

Please send me FREE information on:

☐ Other Books ☐ Speaking / Seminars ☐ Individual Healing Work